Trusting Calvin

Max and Calvin

TRUSTING CALVIN

How a Dog Helped Heal a Holocaust Survivor's Heart

SHARON PETERS

LYONS PRESS
Guilford, Connecticut
Helena, Montana
An imprint of Rowman & Littlefield

Lyons Press is an imprint of Rowman & Littlefield

Distributed by NATIONAL BOOK NETWORK

Library of Congress Cataloging-in-Publication Data is available on file.

ISBN 978-0-7627-8061-7

Printed in the United States of America

To Caroline and Will, enthusiastic young readers, special spirits, and animal lovers, who will undoubtedly become fine citizens of the world.

PROLOGUE

This was it, then—the way it would end after all the awful months and all the grim possibilities threatened and imagined. Here in the near-dusk under a canopy of chestnut trees not yet in full leaf, the darkness of night creeping forward.

The young man, a teenager still, small and impossibly thin, trained his eyes at his shoes, as required. Eye contact was forbidden, he knew. Each of the other four men lined up next to him, shoulder to shoulder, trembling, were aware of this rule, too, and they all stared at the ground.

Death might not be so bad, he thought, attempting to calm himself by retreating inside his head, a safe, quiet place where he could stay until the moment he would breathe no more. The effort failed. He remained excruciatingly aware. He could hear the rustle of crisp uniforms and the cheerful cocktail talk of several people, ten, maybe, or fifteen, clustered not far away, a few of them women, one wearing a dusky perfume that fluttered into his nostrils when the breeze blew in a certain way. They all seemed quite gay, these people, enjoying the evening among the trees, a short distance from the big house, where the festivities had begun.

A voice suddenly soared above the rest, insistent, hard, glazed with the confidence and authority of a man accustomed to being obeyed.

He was pleased, the commandant declared, that this honored group of people had seen fit to join him, these being trying times of such enormous gravity that it was difficult for anyone to manage a few hours of diversion. He had, therefore, arranged for some entertainment, very special entertainment, befitting the auspiciousness of the occasion.

Some of the guests chuckled knowingly.

The soft rustle of movement, the swish of tea dresses, a few words whispered or spoken drifted about as the audience slid into better spots. The silence that followed tingled with a sense of expectation.

"Toten sie!" the commandant finally bellowed, raising his arm and pointing at one of the five tattered men in the ruler-straight row.

The kill command.

A massive German shepherd lunged forward and grabbed the designated man by the throat.

The roaring of the dog, the screams of the man, and the sloppy wet noise of a neck being ripped open filled the air. The sharp scent of blood, coppery and sickening, rose up.

The dog seemed to need no encouragement, but several guests offered it, cheering him to greater ferocity. It continued for what seemed a very long time, this unholy concert of growling, gagging, and gasping.

"Good dog," the commandant said at last, pride edging his voice, when it was clear the entertainment was dead.

Silence fell over the clearing.

Probably I will be next, the young man thought, the next to die in this way. A gun to the back of the head, even with the requisite pre-death humiliation of stripping naked to fan the guests' enjoyment, seemed preferable. Quicker at least. But a prisoner was never given the choice of how to die. Everyone knew that.

Seconds clicked by . . . slowly, agonizingly slowly, as the eyes of the commandant studied each of the four, one by one.

The young man could hear the prisoner standing closest to him swallow repeatedly, probably forcing back vomit or bile that fear had launched from his gut.

"Go. Take them back," the commandant finally spat.

"March!" the guard snapped at the men, still in formation but for the gaping empty spot.

It was hard to make his legs work, hard to believe he was alive.

TRUSTING CALVIN

One

The phone has been ringing all morning, shrill and insistent, breaking into the torpor of August in Cleveland. Routine calls from friends, mostly—two inviting him to lunch, another seeking a recommendation for a good page-turner. He's a voracious reader with no patience for lax literary efforts, and his recommendations are much sought-after.

Two of the calls are of a different sort, however—a high school teacher hoping to snag him to speak at an autumn assembly, and a rabbi asking him to participate in a discussion group.

Max (né Moshe) Edelman is by no means famous, but people are beginning to seek him out, as he is someone with information few can speak about with firsthand knowledge, information that until recently only a tiny handful of people knew he possessed.

He stores the speaking dates in his head, where scores of phone numbers, addresses, and important dates reside, and allows himself a small, uncharacteristic grin of satisfaction. Not because he seeks the spotlight. He is, in fact, a guarded, private man, mostly because of a past so vile and tortured he has for decades closed it—and himself—off, containing the pollution as best he could. Still, it is important to keep busy, and also to share what you have to share, and he's pleased that with these upcoming appearances he might be taking the first tentative steps toward fulfilling a request made of him decades ago in a very different place and circumstance.

Brisk and disciplined in all his pursuits, Max will not go suddenly idle merely because he has silver hair now and recently left his job of almost forty years.

"Retirement is a time that, if handled properly, can be even more productive than earlier years," he has declared more than once.

He has strong opinions about most matters and little restraint when it comes to sharing or living them, so it's inconceivable that he wouldn't have had one about this phase of his life—that he would have let his retirement advance in its own capricious way, buffeting him about like a bird riding the updrafts. He has many plans.

"Max, Steve just called," his wife, Barbara, announces from the kitchen. "He and Janet will be coming by later with Hannah."

Another smile emerges, broad this time. Hannah is his first grandchild, just weeks old, and a greater gift he cannot imagine.

"Very good," he says. "We may go for a walk if it is cool enough."

He speaks in the spare, almost formal manner of people from a certain part of the world who learned English later in life but learned it well, and see no reason to squander the words they have collected. And, in any case, he dislikes chatterers, people who disrupt the quiet with nonsense and prattle. He has never been inclined in that direction himself, believing that sharing a few carefully constructed ideas or a well-told story has more value than babbling about every passing thought. He sometimes wishes others behaved similarly.

Max clicks off the radio, having learned little from the newscast except that all over the city today, tempers are short, and the oppressive heat, bad even by August standards, is causing strange things to happen. Here in the modest townhouse, however, the mood is as steady as ever. Industrious. Tenacious. Composed. Qualities husband and wife toted resolutely to this country decades ago, along with the sum of their earthly possessions folded into two suitcases.

But now the air shifts a little. Max hesitates before asking the question always close to his lips these days.

"How does Calvin look to you today? Better? Worse?" he asks his wife as she settles into a chair across from him to work on an afghan she is knitting.

"His face, it looks sad to me, Max."

Just as Max had figured.

Calvin is, at this moment, off on his own, as he often is these days, curled into a tight circle, as if the only comfort he can find lies deep within his own bones. Heart-wrenching, the unhappiness there.

Big, handsome Calvin, polite and good-natured, with a vein of goofiness coursing just beneath the surface, had worn the typical Labrador retriever expression of perpetual joy every moment of his two and a half years until he had arrived at this house. Then it had withered, fast and fully. The sparkle that once lit his eyes as if some merry mischief-making was always being remembered or plotted has faded. His big baritone bark has gone puny, halfhearted. Everything about him, in fact, seems flatter, duller.

The dog is not sick; he is unhappy—and nothing seems to lessen that.

That Max cannot actually see any of this, having been blind for nearly fifty years, doesn't make him unaware of the descent. Calvin has been losing weight; his movements are slower, less fluid. A man doesn't have to have sight to know these things.

At the root of all this lies one issue: Calvin, exceedingly well-mannered and impeccably well-trained, cannot bring himself to work for Max. He cannot force himself to do what generations of meticulous breeding and thousands of hours of careful nurturing and instruction have prepared him to do—serve as Max's guide dog. Be the sight Max does not have.

"I know he is miserable about this, Max," Barbara has said. "It's written all over his face."

A dog of this sort needs to work, Calvin perhaps more than most. From almost the earliest moments of roly-poly puppyhood, coffee-colored Calvin had distinguished himself with his unflappability and love of learning new things. When he finally grew into his huge Lab feet, an adolescent of unusual conscientiousness, no one had the smallest doubt that he possessed a work ethic even beyond what is expected to become a gifted guide dog.

"That dog simply will not allow himself to be drawn into any drama that's going on around him," Jan Abbott, an instructor at Guiding Eyes for the Blind, where Calvin was trained, had observed. The kinds of distractions or upsets that caused his young kennel mates to lose focus for a moment and tumble around with each other in happy abandon didn't induce Calvin to do the same. If he was in the middle of a task, whatever the task, he kept with it, even when very young, much sooner than anyone expected to see that kind of self-control.

Calvin had sailed through the rigorous assessments and training, demonstrating the temperament, willingness to learn, robust health, and intelligence—tried, tested, and proven repeatedly—to partner up with a blind person. No challenge or circumstance could dampen his love of work, and it had been a perfect pairing, trainers thought, uniting this purposeful dog devoted to doing things by the book with this wiry, nononsense man who shared those qualities.

Calvin hasn't lost that zeal for work, Max knows. Calvin has lost the will to do it for Max.

When they exit the townhouse for a walk, Calvin stands still as a statue at the sidewalk, refusing to move forward at Max's command. Sometimes the dog drops to the ground and hugs the sidewalk as if it's the only safe place in all the world. No amount of insistence, cajoling, or encouragement can convince Calvin that taking Max anywhere is a good idea.

The experts at Guiding Eyes for the Blind have counseled the man. Calvin hasn't been able to feel any sort of bond with Max, they have said, and they suggested many ways for Max to alter the way he acts toward, speaks to, and relates with Calvin so the dog will know that Max likes him, believes in him, and wants to form a connection with him. In a guide-dog team, each side must feel respect and trust, given and received, and when that's missing the work stalls.

It was good advice, precise actions for a precise man to follow, and he did, to the letter. He knows this dog, his first ever, is not at fault. The essence of this problem lies unpleasantly inside himself, like a tangle of weed roots extending into places they have no business being. And he has worked hard to build the bridge across that mess so Calvin can feel the kinship the trainers have said was necessary for him to do his job.

But all of Max's list-making and deliberate actions haven't fooled Calvin. He hasn't been convinced Max is presenting a sincere invitation into the kind of relationship required if man and dog are to work as a team.

Calvin understands how relationships with people are supposed to feel, and the one he has with Max isn't right. When Max pets him, he feels cool reserve. Max doesn't act around him as most people do; he maintains a distance as long and icy as a January river.

So Calvin sleeps today, as he does most days. More than any dog his age should.

"Everything I am doing is exactly as the trainers instructed," Max says, "and yet this."

That all he had counted on, worked for, tried to overcome could be extinguished by this—the emotional needs of a dog—is almost unbelievable. But this is an animal with thousands of dollars of breeding and training behind him, Max knows, and the waiting lists of people desperate for such a dog are long. Perhaps it would be best, he thinks, not for the first time, to give up on this folly, send back the dog for reassignment, and return to his white-tipped cane. The cane doesn't give him the freedom of mobility that it gives so many other people. Max has never become as accomplished with it as some people do, and it doesn't allow him the kind of go-everywhere retirement he had envisioned when he had sought out a guide dog. It's *something*, though. Maybe it is the something that he will have to rely upon after all.

"This dog Calvin just does not want to work for a man like me," Max says at last. "Calvin wants me to be the person he wants me to be, a different person than the way I am. I don't know if I can be that person."

The words surprise his wife. Max doesn't often share concerns he might have about falling short in some way.

The heavy hush of disappointment fills the room.

Max had always been able to analyze his way through impossible situations—imagine the facts on a ledger and devise a strategy that, if not perfect, would resolve the problems he faced. This one has remained stubbornly unsolvable.

"I am afraid," Max says at last, "that I might have reached the end of the road with Calvin."

Barbara abandons her knitting, and studies her husband, the unhappy slope of his shoulders.

"No, Max," she says. "No, you have not. Much bigger challenges you have overcome. This road goes a little bit farther."

Two

The summer of his sixteenth year, the steamy final weeks before events would change everything, Moshe Edelman was unsettled. Life, he knew, would soon propel him toward the responsibilities of adulthood, as life always did in small-town Poland in the 1930s. And it was impossible to know just how all of that would unfold.

He was itching for some clarity.

Uncommonly handsome, with dark curly hair, fine features, and a slight build, he had just begun to feel the insistent stirrings of approaching manhood, and this, he thought, might lead to something as yet unfathomable. Equally tantalizing was the notion that sometime soon, arrangements might finally be formalized that would land him thousands of miles away, on another continent, to begin studying for a career.

"This path of mine, whatever it is, I want it to reveal itself soon," Moshe declared abruptly, shattering the heavy silence of the afternoon. He and his best friend, David, had made their way to the bank of the Struzka, hoping to catch a breeze, and were idly studying the current as if the answer to some universal riddle was being carried along. "A man should not just drift."

David snickered. Moshe's impatience in all matters was well known. He was always one foot or sentence in front of everyone else, and they all knew, all of his friends, that time-wasting and ambiguity annoyed him.

"You'll have to be like the rest of us this time," David said, goading him a little, as best friends can, "and wait for what comes your way."

Having finished his schooling at age fourteen, as was typical of those of his station, Moshe was apprenticing as a salesman in his brother-in-law's clothing shop, work he found tedious, mind-numbing. He fully understood, as his parents had taught, that the worth of work had nothing to do with the pleasure it might bring but rather with the honor that comes from doing something well and making a living. But this fetching of fabrics and adjusting of shoulder seams didn't suit his constitution.

Serious-minded and exceptionally bright, even as a young child, Moshe was, his mother, Sarah, believed, destined for something of significance. She had been pressing on his behalf for months, writing letters, tucking away cash, exploring every possible means to get this son, her youngest, across borders and seas to her sister in Colombia, where eventually he could enter medical school.

"Always I hope, every day, that the mail will bring the documents," she said, as Moshe entered the family home that August evening, having found neither breezes nor answers at the river. "But again today, Moshe, they did not arrive."

Sarah was seated, as she often was this time of day, at her little black sewing machine positioned near the window to catch the last of the waning light, her right hand working the silver wheel that caused the needle to stab into fabric, her left aiming the torn shirt beneath it, sure and true.

Moshe had caught a small twist of worry in her words, and he moved close to turn the wheel for her, the two of them doing the work together, well-practiced, content in their closeness. Theirs was not a family given to physical or verbal expressions of affection, but the love was deep and never doubted.

"I am praying to God every day to get you out of here," she said.

The threat of war roiling over Europe—maybe only eighteen to twenty-four months away, most thought—made exiting Poland complicated, but Sarah clung to the hope that Colombian officials would grant the visa, that Moshe could leave before his eighteenth birthday, at which point he would be forced into mandatory military service.

"Well. There is enough to be done each day without thinking about things we cannot control," Sarah said suddenly, pushing herself up from the chair. "The papers will come in their own good time."

Again, the worry in her voice, Moshe thought. It was there so often these days.

The vague underpinning of tension that had been part of his parents' being for as long as he could remember had been escalating, and he knew it wasn't just because of the distant war and his eighteenth birthday. Many of the elders in town, in fact, seemed preoccupied, often engaging in hushed, worried conversations, the content indecipherable but the tenor so intense he could almost smell the stench of fear that rose from the words like smoke from a wood fire.

But each morning, Moshe's parents arose before dawn, as always, fixed their faces into neutral expressions, left the small house on their well-kept cobblestone street, and walked the hard-packed path to their milling business a few yards away. There they spent the next ten or twelve hours grinding flour and the buckwheat cereal called *kasha*.

It was important work. And the Edelmans were relied upon. Almost as much as they were reviled.

Jews in Krasnik, the Edelmans among them, had initiated and now conducted much of the town's commerce: the dry goods store, tailor shop, bakery, and pharmacy. But whatever small courtesies the townsfolk extended to Jewish merchants during the direct exchange of money for products were fleeting. At all other times, the Jews of Krasnik, all four thousand of them, were treated not so very differently from the vermin that arrived in waves from the nearby fields every autumn. Even from childhood, Jews and gentiles alike understood that.

Jewish boys learned while still in short pants to walk fast and purposefully through town after school to avoid being jumped and beaten. Jewish girls skirted doorways to avoid the young bullies who knotted menacingly to yank up their dresses, a practice intended to humiliate them in the rawest way an eight-year-old can contrive.

Even adult Jews walked with caution through the streets, though their precautions didn't always accomplish much. They were often spat upon, slapped, or beaten.

"I despise this place," Moshe said to his two-years-older brother, Yankel, that summer after a venomous outburst from a Catholic neighbor. "They will never change, these people. We must leave this behind somehow."

There was rarely more discussion than that, among the Edelmans or any of the Krasnik Jews, about the difficulties of their existence. Anti-Semitism had flourished in the town for every one of the fourteen generations reared there since Jews had received the official right to settle in that part of Poland in 1584. Discussing a truth as old and as tenacious as this accomplished nothing.

And the fact is, the Edelman family—father Abraham, a smallish man with chestnut hair, gray eyes, and the long, full beard of Orthodox Jews; Sarah, slim and dark-haired, ten years younger, an arranged-marriage bride; and the five children born to them from 1907 to 1922, when the last, Moshe, arrived—lived a somewhat better life than many Jews. They had their own home, inherited from Sarah's mother, and their mill, which provided a steady if modest income.

Life in Krasnik, situated in rural eastern Poland and surrounded by flatlands planted with rye, barley, and oats, moved more slowly than it did in some other towns. By the 1930s, however, the population had grown to 18,000 people, and most of what a person or a family required was available there. There were several brick municipal buildings, a hotel, clothing shops, cabinetmakers, a butcher, bakers, a synagogue, a Catholic church, an elementary school, and a Catholic high school.

Three townspeople owned cars—an army major, a doctor, and a Jewish entrepreneur who used it as a taxi to ferry people to outlying areas or to the train station. Once in a while an airplane flew overhead, a rare-enough event that nearly everyone dashed outside at the sound to look up and follow its progress across the sky.

Tuesday was market day in Krasnik, the day that farmers from miles around loaded their grain, chickens, cheese, and eggs into wagons and made the trip to town in the gray light of dawn. An especially busy day at the Edelman mill, it was the one afternoon that the Edelman children could escape their tightly regimented schedule of school, study, and religious instruction in order to help out.

Life was hard, and work was constant—not just at the mill, but at home. Water still had to be carried from a source quite distant from the house, and wood was cut at the end of every summer and stacked in the woodshed for the wood-burning stove, the only heat source during the brutal winters that inevitably shouldered autumn aside long before anyone was ready and then lingered stubbornly. The family spent long autumn evenings slicing apples from their orchard to dry in the oven and chopping cabbage to fill a fifty-gallon barrel with sauerkraut. Sarah put up huge stores of peas and beans that she raised in her garden and bought a six-month supply of potatoes and cabbage in September to cram into the stone cellar under the woodshed for the frigid months.

They lived a frugal existence, but whatever the sacrifices required, Abraham and Sarah arranged for each of their children to receive at least a basic education. Until 1925, public education wasn't compulsory in Poland, and was, therefore, all but inaccessible in remote areas. Illiteracy proliferated. The eldest two of the five children, Frieda and Zalmen, were into their teens before the mandatory-education law passed, so Abraham and Sarah engaged a private tutor for them and enrolled Zalmen in *chader* (religious school). Daughter Hennia, along with Yankel and Moshe, attended public school every day, and the two boys headed off to *chader* late every afternoon, removing the square, navy-blue hat with a Polish eagle emblem required at school and replacing it with the round, black yarmulke.

Sarah kept a kosher home, and their children accepted that they would devote many hours each week to abiding by and celebrating the ancient traditions. Shortcuts were never permitted in Abraham's home.

On Friday evenings when they returned from temple, the Sabbath dinner of gefilte fish, soup, potatoes, vegetables, and honeyed carrots lasted well over an hour, with much praying and singing. Every Sabbath day, from ten until noon, the family attended prayers at Krasnik's main synagogue, an impressive old building, lovingly tended. After service, Abraham, stern and exacting, quizzed the Edelman sons about the Torah and the Talmud.

The family approached the high holy days with great solemnity and uncompromising adherence to tradition. Before Passover, every drawer, cupboard, chair, and table in their five-room house was scrubbed, every corner behind each piece of furniture cleaned. All the everyday dishes were washed, packed, and taken to the attic, replaced with the Passover dishes. Each family member had a beautifully crafted seder wineglass, and the seder supper lasted at least four hours, as the family sang Passover songs and recited the Haggadah, the story of Passover, from cover to cover.

Moshe followed the religious traditions as expected, but by the time he had reached his early teens he had come to realize that the praying and singing didn't ignite in him the deep feeling that it did in many others. He was Jewish by heritage, and that was important to him, even if he wasn't as devout as some. And he was interested in having a safe way to spend time with others who shared his heritage, so he joined the Zionist Youth Organization when he turned fourteen, as his brothers before him had. Every Friday evening, he and his friends listened to lectures about Palestine and danced the hora under the watchful gaze of the portrait of Theodor Herzl, founder of political Zionism.

It was among these people that Moshe learned some of the details of the increasingly disturbing developments across Europe and across the oceans that had been stirring such anxiety in his parents and the rest of Krasnik's Jews.

Since the ascension in neighboring Germany of Adolf Hitler—as chancellor in 1933, and as head of state *(Führer)* the next year—the situation there had grown ever more alarming. Jewish property was confiscated, Jewish government workers were being dismissed in massive numbers, government decrees were pressing Jews further into the margins, and Jewish religious artifacts were being burned in public celebrations. Reports circulated that the Nazi rules-enforcers—the *Sturmabteilung* (SA) storm troopers, the smaller elite *Schutzstaffel* (SS), and the greatly feared Gestapo—were beating, imprisoning, or killing Jews. More than fifty thousand Jews had fled Germany as soon as Hitler came to power, understanding earlier than most that the man's anti-Semitic rantings were more than rhetoric. Among German Jews who remained, suicide was increasingly regarded as the only option.

Jews across Europe and across the globe were monitoring these reports with alarm, even as much of the rest of the non-Jewish world was ignoring them. There was a strong belief among most countries that interference in another nation's internal affairs was unacceptable. Just as important, a notion prevailed that Jews themselves had contributed much to the contempt and ill feeling leveled against them. They held entirely too many important positions in government, commerce, and other professions—not just in Germany but in other countries—than they should have, given their numbers and their abilities, it was said. They were clannish and had odd customs. Whatever recalibrating was going on in Germany was no doubt for the good, it was believed.

As the 1930s advanced, more and more Jews frantically angled to leave Germany and the countries sure to be overrun when Hitler triggered the war that everyone knew was coming. But the borders were blocked to Jews. No one wanted them. Immigration rules even in America and Canada became ever more strict.

Even before the Nazis came into power, all of the Edelman children and most of their friends had hoped to leave Poland someday, believing, as they had heard, that in some places Jews received better treatment. Many dreamed of reaching Palestine and helping to create the land of tolerance and promise spoken about by the Zionists. Establishing life there would require the backbreaking work of draining mosquito-infested swamps, clearing rocks from hillsides, and constructing something from nothing. Moshe had few of the necessary skills, but he often imagined himself arriving there, creating a life, and arranging for others in his family to join him.

"To live like free men in a free land—this is what I want," he said to his friends as they left the youth meetings, their souls pulsing with the belief that a different way of living might be possible in this land about which they had heard so much.

"The British control Palestine, which makes it impossible. They will not allow us in," David reminded him.

"Now they will not," Moshe agreed. "But some time they must."

Zalmen, the eldest Edelman son, had made his escape from Poland years earlier at age seventeen. Crossing through Germany, Holland, and France, mostly on foot, sometimes jumping trains, he had reached Belgium late in 1929. Once there, without proper papers, securing employment proved extremely difficult. But he was clever. He schooled himself in the ways of avoiding detection and remained in Belgium for seven years. In 1936, however, he was arrested as an illegal alien and returned to Poland, where he was ordered to report to the military draft board and inducted into the army.

Hennia went at age twenty to a *kvutzah,* a Zionist pioneer camp, to learn agriculture, because most of the few entry permits issued were given to Zionists with farming experience. Two years later, she returned to Krasnik with the certificate and the hope of receiving her permit. Denied that, she married and settled in her hometown.

With each passing year and month, the conditions for Jews steadily worsened everywhere in the region, even in remote Krasnik. A Jewish-owned dry goods store, successful for years, went fallow soon after a non-Jewish Pole opened a similar store nearby and *sokols*, members of an anti-Semitic organization, positioned themselves threateningly in front of the Jewish-run shop.

Abraham was attacked one evening while returning home from synagogue, his coat sliced with long gashes, half his beard slashed off with a pocketknife, his face bloodied. When he reported the incident to the police and identified the two young attackers, whom he recognized, the authorities accused Abraham of fabrication, a charge frightening enough to send him nervously on his way and to vow that he would never again complain.

Even the Edelman mill began to suffer, as farmers—to avoid hostilities directed at anyone who "supported" Jews—traveled many additional miles to mills owned by non-Jews. Abraham's answer to this turn of events was to start a small business selling yarmulkes, prayer books, and other religious items from his living room. The income from either one of the businesses was insufficient to support the couple and their two sons, Moshe and Yankel, still living at home, but the combination of both, along with the money that each of the boys contributed, made it possible to scrape by.

By Moshe's unsettled summer, any hope that the family had nurtured of leaving Poland as a group had disintegrated completely. They needed good connections and a great deal of money to bribe officials, and they had neither. But Moshe would get out, they believed. The documents from South America now held the promise of an entire family.

Then, on Friday, September 1, 1939, the dream dissolved. Germany invaded Poland, and World War II began.

As the German army advanced, the roads became clogged with refugees, a swollen, sluggish target for the German air force, which dropped bombs on them and sprayed them with machine-gun fire. The relentless attacks from the sky had the desired effect: Many people, particularly young Jews and anti-Nazi gentiles who had given thought to joining the fleeing refugees, reconsidered.

Five days later, on the afternoon of Moshe's seventeenth birthday, the Germans bombed Krasnik.

"Run! Get out into the orchard!" Sarah screamed as the first bombs fell. It was never clear why she believed this would be safer than staying in the house, but no one questioned her orders, or her authority.

The family huddled under the apple and plum trees, watching in dazed silence as bombs struck the far end of town again and again, engulfing much of it in flames. The acrid stench of burning buildings blew toward them.

"I knew the war would come to us," Sarah said softly. "I just did not believe it would happen for many more months."

As dusk settled onto the burning landscape, Sarah stood. "Come . . . . We will go to the house. We are safe for now. The airplanes will not drop bombs on us in the dark."

Inside, she put food on the table while the rest of the family sat numbly.

Two days later, German tanks that had ground their way across hundreds of miles of Poland fired three artillery shells into Krasnik, demolishing several houses and killing three people. German soldiers, lean men with mean faces, swarmed in, ordering the townsfolk to stay off the streets.

"Now we are seeing the guts of the beast," Sarah said to Abraham, who was praying, the only thing he could think of to protect his family.

The *Einsatzgruppen* (special killing unit) immediately sought out the town's rebbe, its Jewish sage, Yaakov Ben Zucher Dov, and several prominent Jewish leaders, ordering them to desecrate the synagogue and Torah scrolls and to burn the prayer books. When the rebbe refused he was shot, dragged through the streets by his ankles, and discarded like carrion in the square for all the Jews to see.

The soldiers demanded a huge amount of gold and silver to permit the rebbe to be buried in the Jewish cemetery, an act of enormous importance to the Jews, they knew, and most came forward with anything of value—wedding rings, engagement rings, watches. Sobbing quietly, Sarah handed over the necklace given to her by her in-laws on her wedding day. It had been in Abraham's family for generations.

The gentiles of the town quickly made it clear to the occupying troops that they would cause them no trouble, which allowed the Nazis to focus all their attention on the Jews. They turned the synagogue into a horse stable; commandeered many homes of Jews; and issued a directive: All young Jewish men and women were to report to the town square at six each morning to receive labor assignments for the day.

Sometimes the young men were ordered to scrub manure from the floors of their former synagogue, always with small brushes that required them to move along on their knees like insects while their overseers ridiculed them, their heritage, and their religion. Often they chopped wood, hour after hour, to keep the occupiers warm, the cold months just a stiff wind away. The females did the Germans' laundry or cleaned the houses that they had appropriated.

All Jews were ordered to wear six-pointed yellow stars whenever they were outside their homes, and if they neglected to do so they were beaten or shot. A curfew was enacted: Jews had to be off the streets from seven p.m. to six a.m.

Jews began worshipping secretly in houses and apartments, posting lookouts to alert them to any surprise visits by the Nazis. It was risky, gathering this way, but for a time they could huddle together in a prearranged location, taking furtive comfort in their faith and rituals, the cord that bound them together, when nothing else in their lives was as it had been.

Every move a Jew made was monitored by the Nazis, sharp-eyed and self-important, who arrived in larger numbers every day. All had Lugers, rifles, and whips , and they were quick to use them on anyone who resisted or moved too slowly after an order was issued.

Sometimes the soldiers relied on other implements if the timing or the circumstance seemed right.

Moshe had a favorite cousin, Chayale, a smart, sensitive girl with a gentle nature. The two had shared a special connection since toddlerhood, when they had learned to walk together, giggling and bobbling and pulling each other up after one or the other rocked off balance and sent both to the ground.

Chayale had grown into a heart-stopping beauty with long, thick hair the color of a raven's wing, ivory skin that seemed to glow, and a trim body that had started to bud into full womanhood. At just sixteen, she had very little awareness of the attention she drew, too young, really, to pay much mind to such things, too humble to believe it if it was ever mentioned. But the Jewish boys had long noticed her.

Moshe's friend David had recently declared his heart stolen. "It's as if a sculptor created her," he said in hushed, reverential tones. He vowed that when they were both old enough he would take her as his wife.

One afternoon, two SS, barely out of their teens themselves, watched Chayale pass by. They fell in behind her, matching her step for step. She walked faster, and then she ran. When she bolted through her doorway, yanking it closed and throwing her body against it, they kicked their way in.

She cried and screamed and begged them to go, to leave her. They shoved her into the bedroom and ordered her to strip and lie on the bed, leering, touching her in places she had never been touched. Nazi law forbade Germans to have intercourse with Jews, and these were obedient men. They raped her with a broomstick again and again, shouting, grunting, calling her vile names, stirred into a frenzy, shoving their fists into her mouth to still her screaming.

Chayale's twelve-year-old brother, hiding in the closet, as all children had been instructed to do if Nazis appeared, heard it all, his sister's cries growing weaker.

Finally, the girl struggled no more. The two men strode off.

Beautiful Chayale, in a bloody nest of bedding, was as pale as cold ashes, still as a stone in the field. The broom, sticky with her blood, lay at her side.

Word of her murder spread in minutes. Moshe insisted upon going to her, even though he knew the scene would be horrible. He owed her a final good-bye.

—◆—

Everything in Krasnik had changed. Jewish shopkeepers had closed their doors; the Germans had requisitioned everything of value. Work at the Edelman mill halted completely when the few farmers they had managed to keep turned elsewhere in fear. Jews began running out of basic necessities and set up, at great peril, underground bartering networks.

A moment of joy rose from all the darkness when the eldest Edelman son, Zalmen, returned home safely from the army. He had been taken prisoner and held in a stalag after German forces had overrun his unit. Although thin and worn, he was alive, and he had all his limbs.

As autumn lurched into the winter of 1939–40, cold stiffened the air, and the snow was much heavier than usual. Every morning, one hundred or more young Jews, Moshe and Yankel among them, were herded from the town square to shovel shin-high snow from the two-lane road leading to the railroad station two miles away. During especially vicious snowfalls, when a storm dumped so much so fast the shovelers couldn't keep up, they were whipped. Their feet ached from the cold and then went numb. Many men lost toes that winter. Some days when they shoveled, savage winds roared across the fields, forcing the snow into crusty drifts along their route, and their hands and wrists throbbed from the effort of breaking through them. Their trouser bottoms froze into stiff sheets. Cold and exhausted, they were released at six each night so they could walk home and be off the streets by curfew.

One evening in early January, when Moshe and Yankel stamped their way into the house after shoveling detail, Sarah was frantically rolling clothing into bundles and making small piles of valuables.

"By the day after tomorrow, we must be gone from this house," she said, her voice sharp. "The Germans arrived at the door this morning and said the commandant of the city has ordered us to leave the house in forty-eight hours. We must find a place in the ghetto to live. They are taking over our home."

They managed to secure housing: a drafty, three-room apartment without plumbing in a rickety building they would share with nine other people from two families. Sarah arranged for friends in the country to keep the few items of value they still had, mostly jewelry, some silver, and her cherished cut-crystal seder glass, which had been in her family for generations.

On a wretchedly cold morning, gray as steel, they loaded a few pieces of clothing, bedding, and some utensils into a cart to make the long walk to the ghetto. Sarah refused to look back at the house in which she had spent her entire life. She did not cry. She dipped her head against the biting wind and plunged forward.

Conditions in the ghetto rapidly grew dire. Scarce food, overcrowding, and unsanitary conditions invited sickness and disease. Medicine proved almost impossible to obtain, no one had soap, and the town's only doctor had donned a swastika as soon as the Germans arrived and refused to treat Jews. The number of funerals conducted each day grew so large that people lost track of who, among the families they had known since childhood, was still living and who had died.

Sarah took ill, and the family knew, as all families in the ghetto did when anyone became extremely sick, that she would die from lack of treatment.

When Zalmen, who had married and settled fifteen miles away in Zaklikow, received word of his mother's condition, he pulled off his yellow star and made his way through back roads during the night. In Krasnik he located a man willing to transport them by horse and sleigh overnight to Lublin, where a hospital was still accepting Jews. It was a last-gasp attempt, this journey, as Jews were no longer allowed to travel anywhere outside their own towns.

21

"If we're captured, Mother and I will probably be killed," Zalmen acknowledged. "If she stays here, she will certainly die. We'll try to avoid being seen, and perhaps she will live."

As their brother and mother set out into the frigid night, Moshe and Yankel cried quietly, certain they would never see either of them again. Abraham prayed that night and for many days and nights, rarely sleeping, pleading with God to return, if He saw fit, this woman to her family.

A week later, against all odds, Zalmen returned his much-improved mother to Krasnik and slipped back in the night to Zaklikow.

Soon after Sarah's recovery, food ran out completely. While her sons were away on work detail, she disguised herself as a peasant and made her way to the home of the Polish friend who was holding her valuables for safekeeping. Hours later, Sarah returned, having exchanged her silver, crystal, and jewelry for a sack of potatoes, some flour, and a loaf of bread.

"A warning she gives me as soon as I arrive," Sarah told Abraham that night. "I am never to go back there again. Her neighbor is a Nazi sympathizer, and if he finds out she was selling food to a Jew he will turn her over to the Gestapo."

For a time, at least, they had food again.

The small apartment shared by thirteen people was always tense and always cold, and it offered no privacy of any sort. But the insistence of biology commands attention when a young man comes of age, even when he is scared, starving, and exhausted. Moshe became captivated by Hadassah, the daughter of the apartment owner. She wasn't a beautiful girl, but she was smart, she had a sweet, helpful nature, and the geography of their living arrangements as well as the circumstances of their narrowed lives had set into motion an urgent drifting together.

Drenched in the all-consuming longing that emerges when people are stripped of all but the barest of emotion and denied any opportunity

to act upon the feelings that survive, they fell quickly and deeply in love.

Keeping hidden what was ripening between them was vital. Abraham, they knew, would order an instant halt to the relationship if he learned of it. He would not abide romantic dalliances from his sons, and the seriousness of Moshe's feelings wouldn't impress him. Abraham Edelman believed in the kind of carefully arranged marriage that he had experienced in his own life, one that brought him a large family and allowed him to devote nearly all of his time to prayer and study.

The young couple had taken every precaution to avoid detection, they were sure, and they began whispering of a future together.

One evening Sarah asked Moshe to help clean the supper dishes, an unusual request. As they set about the task, Sarah said in a voice that no one else could hear: "Hadassah is a lovely girl." She didn't look at her son when she spoke, and she gave no special weight or emphasis to the words. But with that one sentence she let him know that she was aware of what was going on and did not disapprove.

Surprised, Moshe realized he was also relieved, and he unloosed a whispered confession he hadn't expected to make. "When this madness ends I want to marry her."

Sarah pulled her son close. "You have my blessing."

Pleased that her son had managed to scrape some pleasure from the walls of this cauldron of gloom, Sarah said she would protect his secret and share in his hope.

Moshe believed this wasn't merely a first-love crush born of circumstance and availability. It was true and real. It was so intense that even decades later, as an old man, he would remember Hadassah, wondering how his life might have differed with her at his side, and include her when he spoke *kaddish* (the mourner's prayer).

Winter began to loosen its grip, and talk in the ghetto held that, once summer arrived, the Germans would move on to places more enticing.

The death rate in the ghetto would slow, they hoped, and food would become more available.

Moshe was recalling that prediction one night in early May as he was preparing for bed, thinking about how he and Hadassah might be able to use the softer temperatures that were moving in to their advantage.

Suddenly, the door to their apartment flew open. Two Nazi officers stomped in and swung their rifles in an arc, eyeing the movements of each person. One of them fixed his gaze on Moshe and Yankel.

"Get dressed now, and get out," he ordered.

There had been similar roundups during daylight hours, when Jews not assigned to a work crew had been released to go home and then were gathered at gunpoint when someone somewhere discovered a task that required five Jews, or fifty. But this was different. A night roundup was unprecedented.

Moshe and Yankel made no motion to resist. The ghetto had buzzed for months with tales of the few unwise men who had resisted. They had been immediately gunned down, followed instantly by the killing of several additional family members or random Jews to deter future acts of defiance.

The two brothers, barely breathing, slid into their shoes, grabbed their jackets, and, without a look at their parents, the others in the apartment, or each other, walked outside. A group of men and boys was already gathered, and all forged through the ghetto as directed, collecting more and more until there were three hundred of them.

They were brought to a halt near several parked trucks, tailgates down, ready to accept their cargo.

Quickly the young men were loaded aboard, jammed against each other tightly, their arms pinioned straight against their rib cages like staves in a barrel. The engines growled to life, and under a cold, starless night they lurched off into the dark.

Three

Four trucks packed with young men bumped and pitched along country roads through the night, passing mile after mile of flat fields not yet sprouting crops. They were heading east, that much the passengers could tell, but toward what and for how many miles they had no idea.

The air was raw, as it often is between dusk and dawn when spring has not yet decided to dependably clothe the countryside with dark-hours warmth, and the short jackets Moshe and Yankel had thrown on were insufficient. The heat created when too many people are crammed into too little space dissipated instantly into the night, but the men were so afraid that most of them barely noticed how cold they were.

A silent, malevolent-looking guard with a rifle and a sidearm was positioned at the rear of the truck, and every once in a while the barrel of his rifle clanked against the truck, the metal against metal sounding too loud even against the engine's roar.

The seventy-five men stood shoulder to shoulder, hip to hip, Moshe and Yankel next to each other, a whisper's distance apart, and no one spoke a word. Asking questions of each other or speculating about what the events of this night might mean would accomplish nothing, they knew, and this was not a time to further arouse the current of anxiety thrumming among them into something that could no longer be contained. Another factor was contributing equally to the silence. Each of the young men had, for many years, been subjected often to situations they were not permitted to question or challenge, and this one, while more ominous because of their number and the distance they were traveling, was not so very different. Remaining mute, experience had shown them, was always safest.

Quiet prayers, barely audible, cleaved the silence every now and then, and as the hours grew longer, more such murmurings spilled forth. Moshe wondered if they were being hauled off to the woods to dig their own graves. Such a thing was not unheard of. If they were being transported for another reason, when would they be returned to their families? He had rarely left Krasnik, where he had been born in one of the bedrooms of Sarah's plain clapboard house, and soon they had passed far beyond the greatest distance he had ever ventured.

Moshe had not said good-bye to his parents or so much as glanced at Hadassah when he was pulled from the apartment, and an awful ache of dread about the manner of his departure worsened with each mile. The idea of leaping from the truck and making a frantic dash across the fields entered his head. But that would only result in a bullet to the back, and then the guards would undoubtedly shoot several other men to demonstrate that escape attempts would not be tolerated. They all knew that, every one of the men. So they sat, unmoving, dry-mouthed, as black skies flowed to gray and fields became forests.

It was well into the next day, when the trucks finally ground to a stop and the men were ordered out. They were deep in the country, they could see, but nothing else indicated exactly where, or why. Only a warehouse-like building surrounded by barbed wire and a narrow river interrupted the endless stretch of fields and trees.

Inside the building, rough platforms extended from the walls, and the men understood immediately that these would serve as their beds. They would be in this place for some time, they now knew. No blankets; no pillows. With only about seventy-five platforms to accommodate three hundred people, the quick-thinking among them calculated that they would have to line up four men to each four-foot-wide platform.

They had gone without food or water for nearly twenty-four hours, without sleep for thirty-six or more, and the adrenaline that had braced them through the night had long ago sputtered to nothing. Many dropped wearily onto the planks, unable to generate enough energy to join the nervous conversations sprouting up here and there. Sometime in the evening they each received a tin of watery soup and a cup of water, but no information.

At dawn the next day they were awakened to begin the job they had been brought here to do. The area, they came to understand, sometimes flooded when the rains or the winter snowmelt were especially heavy, so they were ordered to hand-dredge and shore up the river to prevent future flooding. It was unclear why the river overflowing its banks posed a problem here—an area with no population or structures as far as the eye could see—but that was the work, and they were the laborers. They took the shovels and picks and did it.

They learned that they were on the outskirts of Ruda, a tiny bump on the side of the road about ninety miles from Krasnik. And for more than six months they worked there in water up to their knees, twelve hours a day, digging the riverbed deeper. Then they spread loads of trucked-in gravel high and flat like a barrier fence on both sides of the river.

The guards for this operation were not German Nazis, as they had been in Krasnik. These overseers were Poles of German descent, far worse than any the men had previously experienced, much quicker to slash at backs with bullwhips and much more energetic when bashing rifle butts into hunched-over shoulders, necks, and heads. Their enthusiasm for brutality may have stemmed, as some of the men believed, from wanting to prove to the Germans that they could be every bit as vicious as the Germans themselves were. But many, the ones they feared most, seemed simply to derive pleasure from inflicting pain; if they didn't thrash someone every few minutes, they grew glum or, worse, edgy. No one ever pretended that a guard needed a reason to slam his rifle into a man or slice open his back with a whip; it was just part of the experience.

The three hundred prisoners—it was now obvious that this is what they were, so this was how they regarded themselves—ached, nearly every one, in almost constant pain from beatings or whippings. And as summer loped in with a muggy vengeance, their necks and arms and faces grew raw from blisters atop sunburns that never cooled or healed.

But it wasn't the flock of bruises or the seeping sores that caused the most misery. It was the hunger, grinding and constant. Hunger made them light-headed and flimsy. Their stomachs cramped and thundered, indignant and desperate. The men found it impossible to think of anything but the ache in their guts.

They received potato soup, thin and pale, twice a day, a small metal container of it ladled from a huge, battered vat. And at every meal they silently asked themselves the same question: Will my soup be nothing but water, or will it contain a few pieces of potato?

The man with the ladle had enormous power, the power of life and death, really, over every person in the encampment. If a man received only broth without potatoes for too many meals, he weakened and died.

"If it's someone he knows or someone he's decided he likes for one reason or another," Moshe observed to Yankel after a few days of watching the soup distributor, "he dips deeply, to the bottom of the cauldron, and that person gets a few extra pieces of potato. We must figure out a way to befriend him. If we can't do that, we must at least never upset him or offend him."

Moshe worried about his older brother. Yankel wasn't as strong as some; never had been. He had been severely jaundiced at birth, his condition so dire that their parents had delayed his circumcision from the prescribed eight days after birth until he was four weeks old and more likely to survive the procedure. As he grew up he was more sickly than the other children, always had the hardest time when illness ripped through school. He also seemed to be on the receiving end of harm more often than most. One evening, when someone had hurled huge rocks through the windows of the synagogue, one had slammed into Yankel's head, slicing a huge gash and knocking him unconscious. It took three weeks in the hospital for him to recover.

Moshe believed the past was evidence enough that his brother was not suited to the demands of forced labor, and he regularly coached Yankel on survival skills that he developed as time went on. The first of several rules was this: When there is food, eat it; don't save it. Soon after they arrived in Ruda, Moshe ate half of his daily bread ration one night and put the rest under his head for the next day, when with some extra nourishment he might work fast enough to escape at least some of the whip cracks. While he slept, someone stole the bread. Desperate men do desperate things, and all starving men are desperate, he now knew. Survival could hinge on an extra ounce of bread.

Shoes, too, were a vital commodity. They meant the difference between manageable pain and sheer anguish that could bring a man to his knees. The prisoners quickly learned to sleep with their shoes on their feet, or shoved under their heads with the laces tied around their wrists so they wouldn't disappear in the night.

Many of the men at Ruda knew each other, but the building was oddly quiet in the evenings, the men too tired to waste energy on conversation, and too hungry. There was little to say, in any event. They had no idea how long they would have to shovel muck from the river bottom, and they had no idea what would become of them once someone decided the project was done. They knew only that to leave this place alive, if such a thing was even possible, they had to do exactly as they were told and conserve whatever strength they had to meet the demands placed on them.

They worked at the river seven days a week. Every night they had two hours of free time, and during that time they washed their shirts and picked lice off their arms and chests—long, moving armies that multiplied with stunning speed. The men scratched endlessly at the bites and the sores that sometimes festered, oozing a putrid stench.

At nine p.m., after the sun had slipped away, they moved toward the platforms to settle in for what passed as sleep in this place. If one man changed position in the night, they all had to, crammed so tightly together that the slightest motion required the clump of bodies to shift in unison like trees bending in the wind. Sometimes a man moaned in the night or screamed from a nightmare. Sometimes the July and August heat that had collected in the building, so heavy and oppressive, made sleep impossible. Sometimes the scratching at bites became so intense and noisy that it woke others, and they would growl for silence. Tempers erupted from time to time. But exhaustion and lethargy quickly dampened disagreements to fizzled-out impotence, like a sodden blanket tossed over a fluttering flame.

As summer lost its grip and autumn advanced, a few of the men succumbed to starvation. Before they died they showed the telltale signs of near-death that became horridly familiar to prisoners in the months and years ahead: skeletal bodies, swollen faces and legs, vacant eyes.

"He stopped wanting to live, that man," Yankel said after yet another had died. There was nothing judgmental in his tone. It was obvious he understood how easy it would be to take the small step from an exhausted determination to live to a resigned gravitation toward a place of no pain and no hunger.

"Possibly it's true he gave up," Moshe snapped, worried his brother might fall sway to dark thoughts that could pull him under. "But we must continue to do what we have to do in this place. We must believe that when it's finally over, we will be alive. It serves no purpose to think about why that man died or anything else. Often we have seen it, Yankel. The people who think the most are beaten up the most."

One November morning, when the snow had begun to fly, the workers were ordered onto the trucks again, with no notice or warning. New location, different work, they all assumed. Their only concern was whether the work would be harder, the guards crueler, and the food scantier than what they had just endured.

Several miles into the journey the brothers realized that they were heading toward Krasnik. *Was it possible? Had the long, awful summer's labor been all that was required of them? Would they be returned to their families in the ghetto?*

The vehicles stopped not at the ghetto but on the outskirts of Krasnik, at a sawmill. There they performed cold, dangerous work throughout the long winter and into the next spring. Cut the wood. Pile the wood. Load the wood into trucks. They were cutting, piling, and loading huge underpinning ties for thousands of miles of railroad that the Germans were either laying or repairing.

The men didn't see their families. They never left the worksite or the empty warehouse—midway between the sawmill and the railroad station—where they spent their nights. No sleeping platforms existed here; the floor was considered good enough. The men who had wrapped themselves in long coats when they had been rounded up or somehow had managed to acquire one along the way could spread their coats on the floor to cushion their bones from the concrete. The rest of them settled like dogs, shifting and rolling to find the least uncomfortable position.

Their food rations were identical in quantity and type to those at the river worksite.

"Our captors have developed or stumbled upon the perfect formula for what they want to accomplish," Moshe said to his brother one night as they took tiny sips of thin soup, nursing it as long as possible, trying to trick their bellies into believing they were growing full. It was just enough food to keep the men working but little enough to inhibit outbursts, escape attempts, and, ultimately, most feelings or thoughts. Hunger, when it lasts long enough, displaces pride, neutralizes intent, and extinguishes most normal emotion. And that was evident in this group. The Nazis called their captives *Untermenschen*—subhumans. After so many months of severe food deprivation, that was almost how they felt.

As the men became weaker, their diminished strength led to work accidents, injuries, and deaths. A poorly stacked pile of wood ties rolled onto Moshe one afternoon, and a claw of pain dug deep into the marrow

31

of his foot. He could tell by the wavy way his toes moved when he tried to flex them inside his shoe—before the swelling locked everything into place—that some bones had been broken. He settled himself into a fixed position, all of the weight on his good foot, and kept working, trying to conceal the gnarling pain that coiled from toes to ankle. He couldn't allow the injury to be detected by the guards; if they thought he was working more slowly, they would withhold food.

The foot recovered in time, though it was crooked and bumpy and remained problematic for the rest of his life.

After months in the sawmill, in July of 1941, Moshe and Yankel were reassigned to work at the nearby railroad station, loading scrap metal onto boxcars. Trucks filled with metal arrived in an endless line throughout the day, dumped their loads, and returned hours later to disgorge another twisted pile of ragged scrap. The men assumed it was being transported to a mill somewhere, but for what precise purpose, they didn't know.

One afternoon, work halted to allow a train filled with people to pass. Pinched, frightened Jewish faces peered out as the train inched by. Car after car crammed with Jews of all ages.

"Okay, that's enough!" the foreman roared. "Stop looking at them and get back to work, or you'll find yourself on the next train going exactly where they're going."

By now the workers had heard enough bits of rumors about train-loads of people, mostly Jews, hauled away and never seen again, that they assumed places existed—maybe holding facilities of some sort—where Jews were being taken not to work but to be killed. Indeed, the Chelmno death camp, the first of six in Poland where Jews and other "undesirables" were sent to be killed, was mere weeks away from going into operation.

The fact that the prisoners at the rail yard had no access to newspapers or radio reports or contact with villagers who could have provided detailed accounts of what was happening didn't keep them from hearing certain things. Bits of news pulsed through unofficial lines, as if on the wind, from mouth to ear, a single fact traveling through dozens of people and arriving largely intact and truth-filled.

Just as information dribbled in, it also dribbled out in sputtering spurts. While the Edelman brothers were loading railroad cars, Sarah learned of their presence there from a friend, a station worker who had spotted them. She removed her yellow badge and ducked through trees and back roads, a bundle pressed tight against her side, eventually reaching the station worker's home.

"Please," she implored, "see that my sons get this."

The package contained clean shirts, underwear, and socks, and the ration of bread that she and Abraham had received that day. The man did as she asked, and in this way the brothers learned that their parents were still alive.

After months of loading metal, late in the year, Moshe and Yankel were stuffed into trucks again and transported to a camp a few miles northwest of Krasnik. Compared to the makeshift labor outposts they had experienced so far, this one was an architectural gold standard of confinement and intimidation.

Electrified barbed wire, twelve feet high, broken at each corner by a watchtower manned by guards with machine guns, surrounded the encampment: six barracks, a washroom, a kitchen building, and a bare-earth yard with a roll-call square, known as the *appellplatz*. A sign on the front gate announced, somewhat mysteriously: *Jedem das Seine*—"To each his own."

It was Budzyn, a Nazi concentration camp that—although comparatively small—had a proud devotion to rigid application of the rules.

Each of the cement-floor barracks housed five hundred inmates assigned to one of the three-level-high bunks, no mattresses, no blankets or pillows, just wooden boards. During the first years of their internment there, the men wore civilian clothes, often filched from others who had died. Later, when absolute conformity became more important to the people in charge, the prisoners received grayish-blue-striped pajama-like jackets and pants, round hats, and wooden shoes, clothing that served them summer and winter. They learned to hoard any rag or piece of paper they found in order to stuff it into their shoes or line their jackets to provide a sliver of extra warmth during the three-mile march to and from work each day.

The commandant always made sure to be on hand to introduce himself on the day new prisoners arrived. A ramrod-straight man in his early thirties named Reinhold Feix (pronounced Fikes), he was a former barber, with no great intellect, but great loyalty to the Nazi way.

He had a wife and also a young son, and he taught marksmanship to the boy using live human targets. "Point at the nose or the belly, my son," he would instruct the child when he had identified the man to be killed.

Feix's own preferred weapon was a bullwhip he always carried, outfitted with a special metal tip to better flay flesh.

History would record him as one of the most brutal of all the camp commandants.

But these were details Moshe and Yankel, and the 250 men deposited at Budzyn with them that day, wouldn't discover for weeks to come. Feix had a number of other facts he wanted to share on this day.

Smartly turned out, armed as if for battle, the *Unterscharführer*, as he was known in official circles, stood before them, flanked on the one side by his muscular German shepherd—tightly leashed but lunging and snapping—and on the other by Dimitry, a squat, scowling Ukrainian, who, the prisoners quickly learned, served as executioner when Feix was otherwise occupied.

"Anyone who tries to escape will be hanged," the commandant said in measured, detached tones. "If someone escapes and after twenty-four hours is not found, ten people will be shot and the foreman hanged. You

34

will then have the deaths of eleven men on your conscience." Prisoners were to move briskly, he said, show the utmost respect to their keepers, and march in formation when covering the miles to and from work every day.

The men settled into an unvarying schedule. Awakened by shrill whistles at 5:00 a.m., every day but Sunday, they hurried to the latrine behind the barracks, an open trench crossed by boards—not nearly big enough to accommodate three thousand men in thirty minutes, particularly when dysentery or some other bowel-wrenching disorder was racing through camp.

At 5:30 they received a cup of something bitter, brown, and lukewarm, possibly water boiled with acorns or chestnuts, they assumed, intended to mimic coffee. At 5:45 they lined up to be counted. If the number was off, departures were long delayed, and the men had to endure additional minutes of standing at attention, often while being slammed by fierce winds or lashed by pounding rain. After the count, the prisoners marched to work in straight lines, five abreast, through the camp gates and up the miles of road lined by Ukrainian guards and snarling dogs. Feix often rode his big motorcycle alongside the column of workers, angling in and out among them; some days, he rode his perfectly groomed white horse.

The destination was a former munitions factory, a large concrete structure that the Germans had converted into an aircraft factory operated by the Heinkel Company. Moshe was assigned to a group that assembled and welded the wings of airplanes, and this struck him as a job ripe with possibility. When one is involved in the construction of such a vulnerable part of the aircraft, it might be possible, he thought, to do things that could cause a plane to fall helplessly out of the sky. He and the others in his work group discussed the possibilities sometimes at night, always in whispers, knowing that many among the prisoners would, if they overheard, pass the information on to the Nazis for a half a loaf of bread. In the end, they engaged in no sabotage. They had carefully observed the practices and procedures of the supervisors once the pieces left their workstation. Every part was inspected and then X-rayed. Had sabotage been detected, dozens of the workers, including many unconnected to the subversion, would have been killed.

The work here was less physically grueling than the previous jobs, despite the eleven hours at their stations every day, plus the two hours spent marching to and from the plant. But it wasn't without physical punishment. Some of the civilian supervisors and technicians were every bit as demeaning and whip-happy as the camp guards.

At six p.m. the workers lined up for counting again, returned to camp, and at seven received supper—another quart of soup, usually the same as what they'd had for lunch: pallid water with a few pieces of sodden potato or beets. Occasionally, when a workhorse or one of the well-bred horses that the Nazi officers rode through the countryside broke a leg and was shot, the scraps and bones were tossed into the prisoners' soup. The best cuts went to the guard dogs. The men also received a daily ration of seven ounces of bread, dry and hard to swallow, made from sawdust, crushed chestnuts, and a sprinkle of flour.

Nearly every morning, one man—or several—simply didn't wake up.

Soon after Moshe arrived at Budzyn, he saw that the boy lying next to him didn't stir when the morning signal shattered the silence.

"Get up," Moshe hissed, shaking him.

The boy, stiff and cold, had died during the night. Possibly he had been sick for some time; no one knew. Prisoners in the camps always hid sickness, like animals in the wild. Any sign of weakness or even softness, the prisoners had learned, lessened the chance of survival. The guards could detect either from yards away, and once they did, it was only a matter of time.

When someone died in the night, the corpse was left in the bunk, and the prisoners assigned to clean the barracks after the men left for work hauled it across the floor through the yard and to a ditch outside the fence.

The ditch was very long and very deep. It had to be. Many men died there, and Budzyn had no crematorium. The bodies of the men who had died of starvation or illness, or had been shot, hanged, or beaten for some infraction or for sport were dumped tight against each other, like sausages in a butcher case, to keep the amount of space required as small as possible. Once the stretch of bodies was deemed sufficiently long, a thin layer of dirt was flung atop them so the next layer of corpses could be stacked in another row.

One evening Moshe was watching a new group of prisoners file through the gate and realized that he was looking straight into the eyes of his older brother, Zalmen. Stunned, he could think of nothing to say but the obvious. "How did you get here? Why are you here?"

Zalmen's ghetto had been "cleared," as the Nazis were calling the rounding up and shipping off of Jews, and Zalmen had been transported here, he said, his wife hauled off in a different direction. He hadn't heard anything about Abraham or Sarah for months, or anything about their sisters and their families, still in the ghetto fifteen miles from his own. Each ghetto was kept strictly isolated from others, and information exchange had virtually ceased.

As he spoke, Zalmen was scanning and assessing the place, a calculating expression on his face. He had learned a lot about the mentality and methods of people in power during all those months in the army and the stalag, and he immediately set about using that knowledge. He became friendly with the inmates who had been anointed camp supervisors, ensuring, among other things, that he and his two brothers shared the same barrack. He arranged for Yankel, who had been a master tailor in Krasnik, to be assigned to the camp's tailor shop. It was a busy enterprise, making and repairing clothing for the officers and guards, and sometimes special demands required working late into the night. But it wasn't hard labor, and Yankel didn't have to make the daily journey to and from the plant in every kind of weather, which Moshe and Zalmen were convinced he wouldn't be able to survive for long.

In Budzyn, the lice problem was far worse than it had been at the other labor camps Moshe and Yankel had experienced, and the prisoners developed pocks and craters on their torsos, arms, and legs from relentless scratching and digging. The men didn't realize it, but the danger was far greater than infected sores. Lice carry the typhus bacterium, and sickness soon bludgeoned the camp. The disease that during World War I had killed as many as 40 percent of those infected—more than three million in Russia alone—invaded the already-weak bodies of the Budzyn population with chills, coughing, cramps, diarrhea, fevers, and intense joint and muscle pain.

Zalmen was among the first felled. Fever flamed through him. Moshe and his friends forced water down his throat, wrapped cool rags around his head, and when he became delirious, they held him down so the fits of flailing didn't fling him from his bunk. They had no medicine for any illness, and a few had already died of this terrifying sickness.

When the fever finally broke and it appeared that Zalmen might live, the inmate in charge, who had watched the ministrations from a distance, approached. "Tomorrow you do not go to work. You stay here to clean the barracks."

Unsteady, barely able to speak, Zalmen hauled himself off the bunk the next morning when the others left and began scrubbing floors, his head muzzy, his body only vaguely responsive to what he was demanding of it. Feix appeared as part of his daily routine of inspecting every building to demonstrate that he knew all, that secrets could never take root under his command. He saw Zalmen moving slowly and, enraged at this insolence, drew back his whip again and again.

When the prisoners returned from the plant that evening, Zelman was still working, his shirt and his back shredded, his trousers splattered with dried blood. Again his friends turned to the only form of treatment available, cold compresses.

The next morning, Zalmen joined everyone else on the march to work. Prisoners who didn't recover quickly, being of no value, were shot.

Typhus lingered over the barracks for weeks like a malevolent mist. Moshe fell ill with a case less severe than Zalmen's, though bad enough to leave him partially deaf in one ear.

In two months, hundreds of men had died, their bodies hauled off to the ditch. This unanticipated burst of additional deaths did not create a manpower issue, however. Feix merely had to send word that he needed a hundred more Jews, and a hundred more Jews would arrive in short order. Still, having sick men around was an annoyance. The commandant grew weary of men dropping dead on the job, tired of the stench of dying.

One morning he ordered the barracks where the sick were recovering emptied. Dozens hobbled, as ordered, to the edge of the ditch, and were shot, one by one. This was much more efficient than having to haul corpses across the yard when men died in their beds, and Feix seemed pleased with his solution.

The determined typhus rampage finally slowed.

One early evening as he made his way across the yard toward the barracks, Moshe was deep in thought. Somehow, against all odds, he and his brothers had survived a winter in Budzyn. He and Zalmen had marched through blinding blizzards driven by winds so harsh that ice had formed on their faces, through snow so deep that their feet and legs felt numb all day. Now spring was teasing the camp with the promise, if nothing else, of an easier march to work once the ankle-deep mud from the almost-daily rains, straight, heavy, and sullen, had dried. They were still alive, and he wouldn't have predicted that when winter had begun.

Suddenly a guard pointed his whip at Moshe and motioned for him to approach.

"And you, too," the guard shouted to another man, "and you, you, and you." When he had collected five, he ordered them into formation and marched them out the gate toward the commandant's house. The sentries at the gate smirked and hooted as they passed.

Darkness hadn't fallen yet, though the sun was dropping low in the sky, soft against their backs as they walked toward something they knew would be awful. Feix had been entertaining special guests, they knew, in the same way—through the rumor network—that they knew about much of what transpired in the primly landscaped world the commandant inhabited, far from the stench of latrines and sickness and desperation.

When he entertained, the commandant took pride in providing unusual diversions. That would be the function they would serve, the men knew. There had been stories. This wasn't the first time that randomly selected men had made an early-evening journey to Feix's place. Only four of them, if that, would return to the camp. The only question was by what means one or all of them would die. It wouldn't be a quick death—that much was certain—as a quick death has insufficient entertainment value.

The walk seemed to last forever, yet when they arrived at the spot where they were ordered to form a line it seemed to Moshe that they had arrived too fast. He hadn't had the time or ability to recall all the important memories he had always imagined he would want to relive if given a few minutes warning before his death. He could no longer call up the planes and the shadows of Hadassah's face, and this saddened him. He had recalled too few of the special moments with his mother in her kitchen, the scent of baking apples filling the air between them as she spoke of her plans for him. He had thought about his sisters' babies, their downy heads under his hand and the warm, sleepy weight of his tiny niece as she curled against his chest, but there was so much more about them he knew he should remember.

Time had run out.

Under a soldier-straight line of chestnut trees, the tender leaves not yet mature, whispering against each other in the breeze, the men stopped, their gazes fixed to the ground. They were not permitted to make eye contact with the men and women, a dozen or so, assembled a few feet away making cheerful cocktail talk.

The voice of the commandant rose above the rest, silencing the chatter. He expressed his profound pleasure at the presence of these important guests, promising a spectacle of impressive novelty.

And then he pointed at the prisoner in the center position, next to Moshe, and ordered him to step forward.

"*Kill!*" Feix barked.

The German shepherd at his side leapt forward, grabbing the man by the throat.

The killing of a man by a dog, even by a large, expertly trained dog, is a noisy process, and a long one. The snarling and the shrieking rose into the darkening sky, meeting what sounded to the prisoners like a couple of women giggling nervously.

After some time, the entertainment was dead.

The dog sensed this and released what was left of the man's neck.

"Good dog," the commandant said. The animal was still, but hot, alert, quivering with what seemed to Moshe anticipation of more.

The night grew deadly silent, each prisoner certain he would be the next to die, hoping, actually, to be next, not third or fourth after this.

"Go. Take them back," the commandant finally growled at the guard.

The remaining prisoners turned sharply and began the walk back to the camp at the brisk pace expected, leaving one of their number behind. Moshe hadn't known the man who had died just inches away from him. But he remembered every detail, every second of what had happened. Had he prayed for that man's soul as he died? He couldn't recall. He hoped he had.

He did know one thing. Standing an arm's length away from a long and tortured death changes a person—even here, surrounded by death and dying.

Near the end of 1942, the Edelman brothers received the first piece of information about Krasnik that had crossed the camp walls in many months: All three thousand of Krasnik's remaining Jews had been loaded into railcars and transported to the gas chambers at Auschwitz-Birkenau.

The news came the way all such news did. Sympathetic Poles brought their lunches wrapped in newspaper pages which they purposefully discarded near, but not into, trash cans, so a watchful prisoner could pluck them up. The reports that the prisoners received in this way always circulated quickly, but on this day the information spread with ferocious speed. Almost everyone at Budzyn had relatives in Krasnik—all of them now dead, the prisoners assumed.

"Do not show emotion. You must control yourself," they reminded one another throughout the long afternoon.

That night, the three brothers sat next to each other, silent, all that remained of the Edelman family of Krasnik, Poland. Everyone else was gone, they were sure: their parents, their sisters, and the men whom their sisters had married, the nieces and nephew, so small, so young. Sarah was fifty-five years old and Abraham sixty-four.

Moshe had expected all that long day to feel a wave of grief once he had left the demands of work and the prying eyes of the guards, when he could sit privately and allow his heart to follow its will. But there was nothing. How awful it now seemed to him that he had eaten his evening soup as always, so soon after learning that his entire family, Hadassah, everyone he had ever known, had no doubt perished. Was it possible that his experiences, the horrible things he had seen during these twenty-nine months in the camps, had so fully displaced everything else in his brain that he could no longer feel emotion about something he had not actually witnessed? It would not surprise him if that were the case. He felt little emotion anymore about anything, to be honest, even the things he did see.

He glanced at his brothers, hoping for some sign or spark that would carry him to a reaction that he knew he should be having, but they remained silent, too. Even Zalmen, who always had something of importance to say when circumstances required it, had nothing this night.

The brothers had shared the belief during all the long months at the camp that the misery they were enduring was enough for one family, that it would spare their parents, sisters, and other loved ones. Now they knew no such scorecard was being kept.

—◆—

Moshe and his brothers contemplated escape from time to time, even discussed it occasionally. Such thoughts, however, had to take into account the prospects of post-escape survivability as well as the consequences of success. The results of the few efforts that had been launched had dampened everyone's enthusiasm for such ventures.

In November 1942, three men scaled the fence at the plant and dashed into the woods. Residents of a nearby village found the escapees and turned them in. All of the prisoners were ordered into the yard to watch as Dimitry hanged the three captured fugitives, not in the conventional way, but upside down, to increase their agony. As they dangled by their ankles in the bitter cold, Dimitry slashed at them with his whip. Hours later they finally died, stripes of blood frozen in place on their backs.

"If anyone dares to embarrass me again, this is what will happen to you!" shouted Feix, his face red with fury. "Or worse!"

Still, escape attempts were set in motion from time to time. It wasn't easy for a man to keep within the narrow ground between desperate flights for life and becoming a *Muselmann*, the camp term for someone who had given up. The ditch filled with men who had veered to one side or the other.

A few months after the hanging of the three escapees, another man escaped, and this one was not apprehended. Feix made good on his arrival-day speeches. He picked ten men and ordered them to strip as the entire camp stood at attention. The naked men were marched to the ditch where Dimitry ordered them to their knees and shot them, slowly, one by one. The foreman who had oversight responsibility for the escapees went to the gallows.

Sometimes death came predictably—a rule broken, or a badly timed glance at a guard; sometimes it was random bad luck. One spring morning in 1943, Feix arrived as the march to work was about to begin. He gestured with his whip at first one man, then another, according to no method or reason that seemed apparent, and those men were told to step aside. Soon 105 had been grouped and stripped, Moshe's friend Laibel and his father among them. All were ordered to run toward the ditch. Laibel and his father, in motion, reached toward each other and joined hands. When the bullets mowed them down, they were still grasping each other.

As each new crop of prisoners arrived, additional details about the outside world flowed in, and they learned that the extermination of the Krasnik Jews was merely part of a much bigger program to rid Poland of all Jews for all time. Every ghetto had been or would be liquidated.

Many of the prisoners came to believe that once all the Jews in the ghettos were killed, the Jews in the labor camps—the last of the Jews in Poland not trenched so deeply underground that they couldn't be discovered—would be executed as well. Thus, the arrival of dozens of SS late one afternoon in August 1943 caused alarm. The prisoners were ordered into their barracks without supper, and the doors were barred from the outside.

Moshe stood at a window and watched as SS milled about the fence, inside and outside, clustering, heavily armed, a group here, a group there, some smoking, some talking.

"This is the end," one of the prisoners said softly.

A few men began praying, and several more drifted toward them, a corner of prayer that grew larger and louder. Others sat apart from the praying, as Moshe, Yankel, and Zalmen did, and spoke of their families and of dreams unrealized. A few cried quietly.

The inevitable had finally arrived. Tomorrow they would all be in the ditch.

"This part, the waiting, is worse than the dying," someone said. Moshe agreed.

The hours ground on, the Nazis still massed and huddled outside, the sluggish passage of time almost unbearable.

At five a.m. the next morning, the sound of the bar being lifted from the other side of the door shook the prisoners into full alert. They rose, some reaching out to give a final pat on the shoulder to a friend, moving forward to face what they knew they had to face. When they emerged into the early-morning gray, expecting a spray of gunfire, the yard was empty. The SS had gone.

A shout rang out from a tower. "Go to the washroom, go to the outhouse, and get ready to go to work."

The prisoners learned later that day that the Nazi high command had ordered the Budzyn prisoners killed. But the executives of the Heinkel plant, informed that their workforce was about to vanish, begged officials to reconsider, arguing that these particular Jews were crucial to Germany's war efforts. Sometime in the wee hours, the elimination order was canceled.

That episode, along with all the other episodes of survival, strengthened the faith of some, made them even more devout. For others, however, the level of cruelty they had witnessed was sufficient evidence that there was no God, and they shed their faith, layer by layer, until nothing at all remained. The extremes of opinion sometimes led to heated words. On the eve of Yom Kippur in the year that Feix had randomly chosen more than one hundred men to shoot, the same year of the near extermination of the whole camp, some of the prisoners in Moshe's barracks ate supper quickly and gathered in a corner to recite the Kol Nidre prayers.

Several agnostics, disgusted, formed their own knot. "Look at them, praying to God who has forsaken us. Commandant Feix decides who shall live and who shall die. They are fools."

Moshe's own feelings were conflicted. On the one hand, his religious upbringing had taught him to love God under any circumstance. Even though he had been less than devout once he reached his teen years, some shards of these teachings continued to prick at him. On the other hand, there was the reality of the last three years. He was too hungry and exhausted to arrive at any meaningful position, but it troubled him, this unsettled business of his faith, worsened, he supposed, by the specter of being killed at any moment.

Even Yankel, the most devout of the brothers, struggled.

"Will it be me next?" Yankel asked Moshe one day. "I don't want to know. But I will not blame those who lose hope or those who lose faith. Who will it be tomorrow? I don't know. Maybe me, maybe not. Can I do anything about it? I cannot. What is the use of believing? There is no use of even talking about it."

⁓

Commandant Feix was reassigned, and the prisoners entertained a weak hope that perhaps the next commandant would be less vicious. But there was no perceptible shift in the level of cruelty.

On April 8, 1944, as Moshe was walking across the yard after evening soup, one man among many in the yard, two guards jumped him. They had no reason to pay him any special notice. Moshe was following the rules, as he always did, blending in, as he always did. Possibly they were bored, the usual motivation for a random beating.

Again and again they brought down their whip butts across Moshe's head. Long after he had fallen to his knees they kept at it. Moshe felt flesh disconnect from bone. He could smell his blood as it filled his eyes. The last clear vision he had was of the two blond guards sneering as they kicked him.

Once the guards had clomped off and it was safe to approach, Zalmen ran into the yard. Moshe was incoherent, his eyes pouring blood, his face already swelling so much that he could barely make his lips move. His ears were raw, almost purple, and his nose was gushing. Zalmen hauled Moshe to his feet and dragged him to his bunk, elevating his head onto a pile of jackets and rags so the torrents of blood flowing from so many places wouldn't pool in his eyes or flood his throat. Friends gathered around, careful not to say too much about how he looked, offering small words of encouragement.

"They are worse than animals," Moshe heard one of them say.

Dr. Forster, who had been a physician in Austria before being imprisoned— always respectfully called *Herr Doktor* by the prisoners—raced to the bunk to stanch the bleeding and assess the damage.

"He will live," the doctor finally said to Zalmen. "He's young, and he will mend. I am, however, very worried about his eyes. The left one has been completely destroyed. With nothing but my bare hands, there is practically nothing I can do for him. God only knows how much he will see with his remaining eye."

Moshe remained on the platform bunk for two days. On the third he pushed himself off to go to work. He had no sight at all in his left eye, and just a small blurry wedge of vision in his right.

If he allowed himself, even for a second, to consider that he was all but completely blind, his stomach clenched into itself, and he knew full-blown panic was near. So he forced his energy into experimenting with positioning his head in various ways so he would know what angle permitted the maximum vision from his one semi-functioning eye. Once he had established that precise position, he practiced, swiveling his head back and forth again and again, assuming it so often that he knew exactly what to do to find it instantly, when a split second might matter.

Having mastered this skill, he decided to hope that as the healing process advanced, his sight would improve.

But the sliver of vision deteriorated day by day. He could recognize some items and some people if he turned his head just the right way and if there was sufficient light. That was the best he could coax from the one eye that still worked.

His friends took to sandwiching him between them when they walked or worked. No one dared wonder how long the charade would work. Moshe would be shot if his blindness was discovered.

Two months after the attack, in June 1944, as the Red Army advanced across Poland, Budzyn was summarily shut down.

The Edelman brothers and most of the other prisoners were taken to the train station, loaded into boxcars, and transported hundreds of miles to Wieliczka in western Poland. Here the Germans' legendary skill for perfect planning failed. The High Command had developed an idea, never fully explained to the prisoners, about placing machines in the salt mines there, presumably to extract minerals. Once the men had been unloaded, however, functionaries discovered that the mines were impossibly wet. No work could be done.

The prisoners remained there for four weeks awaiting further assignment. Officials somewhere, unhappy about the idleness of so many men, decided to make use of the time by formally imprinting their status upon them. Each man was given a tattoo, a hastily needled primitive-looking KL, standing for *Konzentrationslager*—concentration camp in German.

On August 1, they were loaded into boxcars again. As always, they had no idea where they were going. This time, though, they knew that it was as likely to be a death camp as a labor camp.

Four

The men were crammed eighty to a boxcar in the late afternoon, shoulder to shoulder, so tight against each other that no one could move or change position. It was broiling hot, and the boxcars became steamy and fetid, reeking of sweat and bodies too long unwashed. The engine was hauling so many cars that it never picked up much speed; the train just ground into a slow, numbing rocking motion. It was nauseating, this combination of heat and stench and swaying, and many of the men vomited, sliming the floor. They couldn't last long like this, and they prayed the journey would be short.

It was not.

As the sun rose high in the sky late the next morning, heat radiated from the roof and sides of the car. No food, no water. Not even a bucket in a corner where a man could relieve himself. By afternoon, almost a full day after they'd started, bladders and bowels could no longer be denied. A man with a makeshift knife spent hours scratching and digging a hole they could use as a toilet, but it was almost impossible to maneuver their way to the hole, and some passed out making the effort.

The train stopped to take on water and coal for the engine a few times, and during those brief pauses the doors opened, allowing a slice of fresh air to drift in. One bucket of water was thrust forward for the eighty men to share. It wasn't enough—just one sip per man.

On each side of the car, just below the roof, two narrow, grated windows served as a peep crack to the outside. The men who stood near them described the scenery for the men close enough to hear. The summer colors were beautiful: verdant green fields, lush trees, flowers abloom in yellows, lavenders, and reds. When the train passed through towns, the watchers reported, they could see people staring back at the human faces peering out at them. Those people probably knew or suspected where the train was heading—if not the precise destination, then the sort of place it was. And they didn't stare for very long.

Moshe stopped sweating. His body had no fluid left to release. He could almost sense his organs shutting down, one at a time, even though such a thing was impossible to feel, he knew. He was certain he was on the brink of becoming delirious. Maybe he had already reached that point, he thought, but was too close to death to recognize it.

Several men died standing up. Their bodies simply stopped working after months or years of deprivation, this final assault of prolonged dehydration, heat, and hunger one they could not fend off. Each time the train stopped and the men shifted a little, the corpses lost the support from the live men stuffed up against them, and they dropped to the floor.

After three nights and two days on the train, having crossed the border into Germany along the way, though the men didn't know this, the train slowed and then halted again.

There was something different about this stop, they realized as soon as the doors screeched open. A long column of guards stood at attention, watching them, and a camp, much larger than Budzyn, loomed in the distance, nestled among towering evergreen trees and jagged rock faces.

As they seeped out of the cars, blinking hard in the late-morning sunlight, they noticed a queer, heavy odor they had never smelled, but which they identified instantly. It was the stench they had heard of in recent months, the stink of recently burned human flesh, and it glued itself to their skin and nostrils, so leaden and cloying they could almost taste it. This, they realized, almost as one, was one of the storied camps where people died or were killed in such numbers that a burial ditch wasn't sufficient, so the Nazis had built a crematorium to turn humans to powdery ash.

The thought, once registered, slid off, their brains unable to process anything more complicated than the raw, aching hunger gripping their guts and the billowy depletion from standing and swaying for the last three days. Weak and flaccid as fish washed ashore, they moved with as much speed as they could manage toward a makeshift corral, some of them collapsing along the way. There on the baked earth they were stripped of their clothes, no shade or shelter from the fiery sun, left to consider the evidence that pointed to only one outcome: They were destined for the crematorium.

When night fell and the mountain temperatures plummeted, they huddled together for warmth under the eerie silver moon, piles of pale naked bones, shivering, barely human. At daybreak, they were rousted to their feet and ordered to march forward, headed for, they all supposed, whatever instrument of death would be used. Moshe could see almost nothing, just a little shaft of light and vague forms, but he could feel the resignation in the men who surrounded him, and it matched his own.

When they were brought to a halt it was in front of a line of men wearing not military or guard uniforms but prisoner uniforms.

"They have no guns," Zalmen whispered to Moshe.

"My God, they have razors. They intend to shave us. We are not to be killed."

Barbers—"inmate specialists"—shaved every hair from their bodies, head, chest, and groin. Disinfectant to combat the lice that remained was smeared on their armpits and groins. The Nazis wouldn't go to all this trouble, they knew, merely to push them into the ovens.

They were laborers again.

They were finally allowed to dress—in pajama-like uniforms, striped, blue and black. A white strip on the chest indicated the prisoner's number. Moshe Edelman was 14426.

"Memorize it, remember it," Zalmen told him. "It's important."

Next to the number, a yellow triangle indicated that he was a Jew.

Formalities completed, they were assigned to barracks, Moshe, Zalmen, and Yankel to Barrack No. 4, one of sixteen identical structures rising up in determined rows.

They were in Flossenbürg, they eventually learned, built by the SS in 1938 for political prisoners. It had a kitchen, laundry building, and the requisite watchtowers and lights perched high to prevent after-dark escapes. The Nazi enchantment with slogans, so often bizarrely incongruous, was in evidence here, emblazoned on the gatepost: ARBEIT MACHT FREI. *Work shall set you free.*

The facility had been designed to hold eight thousand inmates. By 1944–45 it held more than twenty thousand, most of them political prisoners from the nations of Europe that the Nazis had occupied, as well as German criminals, prisoners of war, homosexuals, Jehovah's Witnesses, Gypsies, and, finally, Jews, who made up only about 12 percent of the population. The overcrowding meant they had to sleep four to a bunk and stand in line much longer than in the past for soup and bread. The Jewish minority in the population meant there was a great deal of anti-Semitic behavior from fellow prisoners.

The food was minimal, the barracks broiling in the summer, frigid in winter, and the guards skilled in acts of cruelty, just as in the other camps. But some aspects of this camp were very different from their earlier experiences.

A torture chamber, which the prisoners called the torment bunker, sat behind a brick fence. The prisoners couldn't see what went on there, but the people in the bunker—political prisoners and prisoners of war—were given food during the days or weeks they were kept alive for interrogation, and the men who carried it to them shared with others what they heard inside.

Flossenbürg housed some of the most important prisoners of World War II: seven spies who had dropped into Germany and were captured, German Resistance leader Wilhelm Franz Canaris, and Dietrich

Bonhoeffer, a revered anti-Nazi Lutheran minister who had helped many Jews escape. Also sent to Flossenbürg for special SS treatment were the six men thought to have been involved in the plot to assassinate Hitler, and famed French Resistance worker Simone Michel-Lévy. Moshe and his brothers were ordered to attend many public hangings in Flossenbürg, events presented with great bluster and milked for dramatic impact.

The crematorium was also an unnerving presence the Edelman brothers had never before had to contend with. A smallish brick oven in a nondescript concrete building with a chimney taller than the building itself, it lay a few hundred yards downhill from the camp's perimeter. Some of the people cremated there had died of starvation or disease, some had been shot or hanged, many had been gassed.

The gas chamber at Flossenbürg wasn't specially designed or attentively constructed like those at the sites that served as extermination camps: Auschwitz-Birkenau, Belzec, Chelmno, Majdanek, Sobibor, and Treblinka. The Flossenbürg "gas chamber" consisted of a big military truck retrofitted to do the job. When it was time to gas several people, the guards herded them into the back of the truck, turned on the engine, and the exhaust slid through hoses to the back where the people stood. They died more slowly in the truck than in the custom-built gas chambers at other camps, but eventually they stopped screaming and breathing.

The prisoners hoisted into the truck, at least in the first few weeks after the Edelmans arrived, generally came from the barrack that housed the sick and ailing, men who didn't recover quickly enough from illness or injury. Later, infractions that previously resulted in being shot—breaking camp rules or not working fast enough—led to gassing. The Germans were trying to preserve as much ammunition as possible for fighting the war.

As time went on, the death rate at Flossenbürg escalated, and the crematorium operated around the clock. Sometimes even that wasn't sufficient, and corpses were piled up like cords of wood, doused with gasoline, and set afire.

The work days were, as always, long and grueling. Some of the prisoners worked at the recently opened Messerschmitt factory, about an hour's walk from the camp, where they built parts for German fighter planes. Others worked at a stone quarry near the camp, an assignment that amounted to most as a slightly delayed death sentence. Hundreds were crushed by falling slabs, plummeted to their deaths after an exhausted misstep, or were ground to lifelessness by the punishing process. As in Budzyn, whenever too many deaths or killings caused a shortage of manpower, another trainload of men from another camp resolved the problem in a day or two.

The aircraft manufacturing factory had been established here in 1943 after the main plant was bombed, and that was why so many of the Budzyn prisoners had been sent here. They knew how to assemble airplane parts and how to work in an assembly team. Here they did the same—producing parts for the Me-109, the backbone of the Luftwaffe, used as fighter-bombers, bomber escorts, and reconnaissance aircraft.

Zalmen and Yankel made sure they were on the same team as Moshe so they could cover for his slowness and mistakes. Moshe positioned himself at his six-person station, felt out the parts, and kept his hands moving. When a guard approached, his friends would whisper a warning, alerting Moshe to lower his head and look especially busy. When he made an assembly error, someone quickly reached over and corrected it.

Moshe had learned to listen for every signal and movement, to walk with a determined step even though he could see almost nothing. He had become so adept at sensing his surroundings and adapting to the slightest pressure from a brother or friend who steered him almost imperceptibly, that the guards suspected nothing. It was nerve-racking, nonetheless, these around-the-clock maneuvers to avoid detection.

After five months in Flossenbürg, Moshe's sliver of vision diminished to almost nothing. He knew the charade couldn't continue much longer. If the guards learned of it, he would be killed, and his friends as well. If a mistake left their station because he couldn't recognize objects, their overseers would assume sabotage, and they all would be hanged. He couldn't allow that to happen. He was not ready to die, but he knew he couldn't avoid it much longer.

It was time.

Moshe sat with Zalmen and spoke fast and earnestly, leaving no room for debate. "If you have your sight, if you have your legs, you can walk, you can see where you walk. You can postpone death—it's possible. I can't see where to walk. Death is coming to me. I don't have to look for it, it's coming, and I refuse to have others die as well, with me, because of me. That would be unconscionable."

"We have managed this long," Zalmen snapped. "We will continue. Live this minute and the next minute and the rest of the day. Work, sleep, and get up the next morning and start over again."

For a few more days Moshe did as his brother asked.

But one morning in early February 1945, when he awoke, the narrow sliver of blurry vision had vanished. He was completely blind.

He had to stop working.

"I can't see any tools," he told Zalmen and Yankel. "You must understand: I cannot risk the safety of the others. My life isn't worth anything anyway. Whatever will be, will be, but I can't go to work anymore. We must report this."

He felt his brothers staring at him, mute, trying to find the right words to say.

Finally Zalmen arose from the bunk and crossed the room to speak with the barrack supervisor, a German gentile named Erich, a political prisoner wise in the ways of survival, who had demonstrated that, although strict, he was fair.

"Moshe can see nothing," Zalmen said to Erich. "He is completely blind. He cannot work any longer."

Zalmen didn't look into the German's eyes as he spoke the words, nor did he ask for leniency. Neither was permitted. Erich looked at Zalmen and then across the room at Moshe. "Go back to your bunk," he said, nothing more.

Zalmen and Yankel didn't sleep at all that long, awful night, knowing their brother would be shot or gassed soon after daybreak.

Moshe spent the hours trying to remember every moment of happiness and peace in his past. He had done what was necessary to remove the others from the jeopardy created by his blindness, and whenever a gust of panic about the coming morning blew through him, he reminded himself of that. Even if by some miracle he somehow managed to survive this hell, he thought, as he lay there in the dark, this life wouldn't be worth living. Completely blind, unable to work or care for himself.

It was done, and it was right that it was done. He had no regrets.

At morning roll call—his last, he knew—his brothers pressed closer than usual.

There was a shuffling sound. Someone had sidled in next to him.

"Go back and get in the top bunk," the voice of Erich said.

Erich had made a decision. He didn't explain it, then or ever. He barely knew this young man named Moshe, but he had decided to protect him, knowing full well the consequences of hiding a blind Jewish prisoner.

When the building emptied for the day, Erich moved close to Moshe's bunk and instructed him on the fine points of continuing to stay alive.

"Flatten yourself on this top platform when the other men go off to work," he said. "The guards will have no idea you're here, and if anyone thinks about you at all, they'll think you're in another unit."

Because Erich was German, and therefore thought trustworthy, his fabrications about Moshe's whereabouts during head counts were never doubted. Whenever officers inspected the barrack, Moshe lay on his back, still as a corpse, not breathing, and just as Erich had predicted, they never climbed up to investigate the highest bunks, careful to keep as much distance as possible between the bedbugs and themselves.

It was an enormous risk, this ruse. There were few Jews in this barrack, which increased the likelihood of being reported to camp authorities. But week after week, Moshe lived silently on that top bunk without being detected, alone all day in his darkness, nothing to fill his mind or occupy his thoughts.

Sometimes Erich, who did not have off-site work assignments, leaned in and spoke softly and earnestly to Moshe. "The only currency you have in this place, the only currency any of us has, is hope. If we give it up, that is the end."

A communist and a student of philosophy, Erich often shared thoughts that he believed could help a young man in a bad situation. He especially liked Friedrich Nietzsche and regularly quoted a favorite line: "That which seeks but fails to destroy you strengthens you."

Moshe clung to those words. When the war was over, he would find an eye surgeon to repair his right eye, the one that had allowed that small wedge of vision for all those months. It must be salvageable, he told himself.

Every evening after his brothers and friends returned from work and had walked him to and from the kitchen for soup, they navigated him around the barracks to keep his muscles from atrophying. Then they gathered near his bunk to talk and share the latest rumors, trying to buoy his spirits.

Survival had for years relied on taking certain actions and avoiding certain others. Now it depended on being completely passive. This passivity was much harder than the previous approach. It lasted for two months, this hard, silent, isolated existence.

Early one April morning, barracks supervisors were ordered to escort anyone unable to work to the infirmary. Erich and Moshe both knew floor-to-ceiling inspections would now be conducted. There was no longer any way to prevent discovery of the blind Jew.

Before sending Moshe on, however, Erich spoke with the infirmary supervisor, a German named Hans, from whom he extracted a pledge to protect Moshe to the highest degree possible. Hans took his promise to Erich seriously, spending time with Moshe every day, trying, as Erich did, to keep up his spirits. This time in the infirmary wouldn't be indefinite, however. Eventually the beds would be cleared of the valueless sick people, they knew. The infirmary was conveniently located near the crematorium.

On the evening of April 15, as Moshe was speaking with a French Catholic priest with whom he had become friendly, a guard flung open the door.

"All Jews are to report to roll-call square in fifteen minutes!" the man shouted.

This evening lineup could mean nothing but trouble.

"Moshe, pretend you are not Jewish," the priest said.

A Ukrainian patient who had overheard the priest snarled, "Hey, Jew, you've got fifteen minutes to get the hell out of here."

The Catholic and the Jew said nothing for a moment. Finally Moshe spoke. "As you see," he said to the priest, "if I don't go, he will give me away."

"You are right, Moshe. Unfortunately, you are right. God be with you."

Moshe shuffled to the door and grabbed the sleeve of a man walking past, assuming rightly that he was headed for the square, and soon Zalmen and Yankel hurried forward to collect him.

"We are leaving camp," an official announced. "Everyone."

With the Allied armies advancing—Americans from the west, British from the north, and Russians from the east—High Command had ordered the prisoners evacuated to Dachau, 140 miles away, though the prisoners learned none of this that night. Similar evacuations to push concentration camp prisoners deeper into the interior of Germany were taking place all over the country—partly to ensure they didn't fall into enemy hands, and partly to ensure a sufficiently large labor force to maintain production of armaments for as long as battle supplies were needed.

Flossenbürg's more than 20,000 prisoners would be moved in a twenty-four-hour period, it was announced, in groups of 2,500. The Jews would go first, at sunrise.

Hustled to the railroad track at dawn the next day, the Jewish prisoners were loaded into several boxcars, crammed once again against one another.

Large red crosses had been painted across the roofs of the cars, a strategy that the Germans had been using for some time. This wasn't to protect the prisoners they were hauling from place to place for war-related labor or to put them to death, but to protect the passenger cars at the rear, loaded with the wives and children of officers who had already been transferred. The trick worked for a while, but by the time this train was departing, the Allies assumed all trains were carrying weapons or soldiers to critical areas and did not refrain from firing on them.

Just a few minutes into the journey, the roar of low-flying aircraft rumbled above the train. Machine-gun fire ripped through the roofs. The men in Moshe's car dived to the floor, a tangle of bodies atop one another, three or four deep. Zalmen flung himself over Moshe, and both landed on another man. When the shooting stopped and the two brothers stood, they realized that the man beneath them was dead, bleeding from the belly. A bullet had ricocheted from the metal rail beneath them, piercing the floor of the car and killing him.

The attack killed dozens of Jews and destroyed the locomotive. The guards who had survived forced the prisoners from the cars and herded them across the field to the road nearby, shouting orders and threatening to unleash the dogs. A few prisoners escaped into the woods, but most were too close to a gun or a snarling animal to make such a dash worthwhile.

Ordered into five-abreast formation, Moshe grasping the arm of Zalmen with his left hand and his friend Shlomo's with his right, hundreds of Jews headed west, heads down, walking to an unknown destination an unknown number of miles away. An hour into the walk, the pop of a single gunshot came from the rear, then another. Soon, the shots were much more frequent. Men too sick or too exhausted to walk, falling down or not keeping pace, were being finished off on the side of the road.

A slow, steady rain began to fall, biting against their faces in the chill, turning the road slick. Moshe let go first of one arm and then the other to pull his thin jacket tighter against his throat, an ineffective shield against the cold. Every few minutes he turned his face upward like a creature of the desert, capturing the only water available to them. The gray skies and steady drizzle seemed to some of them nature's way, maybe God's, of giving them a chance to survive this ordeal.

The first day of the march was almost unbearable. The next day was worse. More marching, more gunshots. Day after day they walked, encountering almost no one, stopping only when the guards needed rest. The men knew, from overheard snatches of guards' conversations, that the other thousands of prisoners from Flossenbürg were also marching along this road, cadaverous men with shaved heads, extending mile after mile.

They huddled under trees in the fields at night, submerged into instant, exhausted sleep. Each morning at first light, they got up and continued walking.

On the fifth day, Moshe could take no more. His feet were raw from poorly fitting wooden shoes, oozing pus and blood. Every step unleashed a whorl of pain.

"This is it for me. I can't go on," Moshe muttered.

"Do you know what day it is today?" Shlomo growled.

"No. I don't care."

"Today is April twentieth—Hitler's birthday," Shlomo said. "You are *not* going to give him your life as a birthday present."

Moshe kept walking.

Zalmen offered his brother his shoes. When Moshe refused, Zalmen removed his own in mid-step, passed them to Shlomo, and approached a guard to ask if he could take shoes from a dead inmate. The guard agreed, and Zalmen returned with better shoes for his brother.

On the seventh night of the march, the guards, wanting to dry out from the merciless rain, directed the remaining men, possibly only 1,500 now, into an empty barn. Having a dry floor on which to rest was sheer luxury.

━━━

"Heraus schnell!" a guard shouted the next morning, April 23, when the barn doors opened. Out quick.

They emerged into the warmth of sunshine, a gift, Moshe thought, that might make it possible to walk one day more, possibly two. They had almost nothing left, but if they were warm and dry they might be able to force a little more from their bodies. They could worry later about the absence of rain leaving them no water to drink.

Just then an airplane flew overhead and a shower of leaflets pirouetted down through the blue skies, landing by the hundreds in the unplowed fields. The prisoners were ordered to ignore them, but each of the guards stooped to grab one. Within seconds, the guards' shoulders sagged. They kept the prisoners marching forward, but without the fervor of the previous days.

"What is this? What's going on?" Shlomo whispered to Zalmen.

"I don't know. Something about the papers has them worried."

"What? What do you see?" Moshe asked, aware of a shift in the texture of the march. The guards would swarm together for a few seconds on the edges of the limping column, speaking in urgent voices that no one could quite hear, then resume their positions.

Soon, the guards directed the men onto a dirt road that seemed to go nowhere. As they moved closer to the woods, some of the prisoners concluded that this was where they would be gunned down, left in bloody piles, and they began whispering among themselves nervously. Suddenly, the guards hoisted their machine guns over their shoulders and ran toward the trees, away from the prisoners, hauling their dogs with them.

"They've left," Zalmen said, amazement in his voice. "The guards have all run away."

The prisoners stood motionless, stupefied. Moshe could hear snatches of the questions that they all asked of one another.

Is it real? Are they really gone?

It's a cruel trick.

Are they joining up with others in the woods so they can gun us all down?

No. I think they're really gone.

Frozen in place, the men couldn't think of what to do next. After a time, they broke into small groups and headed back toward the highway, some looking over their shoulders for a surprise attack from the woods. Drawing closer to the road, they heard the roar of heavy vehicles, a great many, pushing their way along the highway.

"It's the Americans!" someone shouted from up ahead. "We are free! We must be free! That's what those pamphlets were; they were telling the Germans to surrender."

It took some seconds for the men to believe what they were hearing. Some fell to their knees in the soggy field and laughed; some wept. Others, too numb to understand what was unfolding, stood motionless, eyes half-closed, still thinking about the Germans in the woods.

The Americans rolling by in trucks and tanks and Jeeps recoiled at the sight of the skeletal remains of what had once been men, skin sallow and eyes flat, closer to being corpses than humans. The prisoners closest to the highway could see that many of them were weeping as they tossed what food they had in their vehicles to the side of the road for them.

The hundreds of Jews—who had become, in sudden, surprising seconds no longer prisoners but survivors—continued forward. They should not go far, the Americans warned. The front lay just miles away, and danger was high.

Spotting a little farm with a cleared field on the outskirts of a village, which they later learned was Schwartzenfeld, the survivors stopped and collapsed into tired heaps, hundreds growing into thousands as wave after wave of men in tattered concentration camp uniforms stumbled wearily into their midst.

A group of American officers, some speaking perfect German, arrived to organize the mess of men. One noticed Moshe, doubled over on a bench, ashen, stricken, and helped him and several of the sickest men to the farmhouse, directing the woman there to serve them the tea and crackers that he gave her.

"Make them as comfortable as possible," he ordered the woman, who was obviously unnerved by the sudden appearance of foreign soldiers and unhinged by the men who didn't seem like men at all.

Throughout the day, the officer returned to the farmhouse often, concern etched in each word he spoke. "I am trying to get you to a hospital," he said to Moshe. "It's complicated because we are so close to the front, and there are no vehicles available to take you, but we're working hard on it."

Zalmen and Yankel came to Moshe's side several times to tell him what they were seeing and hearing. Survivors were arriving by the hundreds, and food was being cooked on campfires. Tales circulated of thousands of men shot on the side of the road during the Flossenbürg march, prisoners who almost made it but had fallen a few hours or a few minutes too soon.

Historians eventually pieced together from scanty records, survivor testimonials, and body counts that about 22,000 prisoners marched out of Flossenbürg, and about 7,000 of them dropped dead or were shot along the way.

The Americans told them that theirs was not the only forced march through Germany. Reports were coming in of many others—death marches, they were calling them—from concentration camps scattered around the country, tens of thousands of men and women, all of them closer to death than life.

Early in the evening, Moshe sat by an open window listening to the men and machines milling about outside. His hunger satisfied for the first time in five years by a handful of crackers, he was beginning to recover, after hours of sipping tea and water, from his severe dehydration.

But he'd had to ask how to get to the washroom—just a few steps away, it turned out—that he could not see. He could hear the moaning of another survivor, but he couldn't see if there was any way he could help. When the woman of the farm had placed a cup of hot tea before him, he could smell it, even feel its heat, but he couldn't reach forward without fear of knocking it over.

I may be free, but I am blind, he thought.

His whole family was no doubt dead, except for the two brothers who had formed a wall of protection around him that had not fallen. He had no home and few friends. He was now twenty-two years old, and he had no idea how he would ever be able to take care of himself. He could speak five languages—the Polish, Hebrew and Yiddish of his youth, and the German and Russian he had become fluent in as a survival tool in the camps—but he couldn't earn a living. He had withstood monstrous cruelty and deprivation but was utterly incapable of performing simple tasks. He began to weep.

The door to the farmhouse opened, and Zalmen announced in a cheerful voice, "You have company."

A man swept Moshe into a bear hug. "We made it! We have survived. We are free," Erich exclaimed. Pulling away, the German noticed Moshe's tears. "You're crying. Are you in pain?"

"No, not that kind of tears," Moshe said between heaving sobs. "I have survived, yes. If not for you and my brothers, I would have gone up in smoke."

That so many others had been hurled into the crematorium, dumped in ditches, or kicked to the roadside and shot when they could march no more—every one of them capable of making more of a life than he himself would ever manage now—made no sense. It wasn't right. It was unbearable.

"I don't know whether I should thank you or despise you."

Five

Awakening on the floor of the farmhouse as a free man for the first time after 1,795 mornings as a captive in one camp or another, 140 more as a prisoner in the ghetto, Moshe felt disjointed. He should have felt relief and gratitude, he knew, but whatever layers of his being that might have contained those emotions had dissolved somewhere along the way.

In the camps he had gone from naive teenager to twenty-two-year-old man, propelled ahead like trash on a slow-moving creek, floating toward nothing known, barely conscious of the passage of time. Everything had been specified, scheduled, presented, or withheld according to some scheme he had never understood and couldn't question. What does that do to a man? He had no idea. He did know one thing for certain, though: He was blind. He could look forward to a life as a nuisance.

Yankel, Zalmen, and the three friends who had slept near Moshe in the farmhouse stirred. Their first words of the morning revealed that for all of them, the euphoria of the day before had given way to an uneasy understanding that they, too, were unprepared to assume their places in the world again as normal human beings.

"We have lived for five years like draft horses on a farm—fed by someone else, whipped into compliance, trained to perform so they would feed us," Yankel said. "Now we don't even know how to find bread, how to pay for it. Our ability to care for ourselves has been stripped away."

They were hundreds of miles from their hometown. Their family and friends in Poland, the means by which generations of Jews had glided into employment, had all died. If they possessed any useful skills, they had no idea what they were, and they believed the resentment toward

Jews would be even greater in post-war Europe, dimming their prospects further.

Their best hope, they concluded that morning, was to get to a city where some opportunities might exist, a city where there were also doctors who could examine Moshe's eyes. They would leave immediately, in an effort to arrive ahead of the waves of survivors who would undoubtedly surge in once they had recuperated sufficiently in the displaced persons camp being established nearby by the United Nations Relief and Rehabilitation Administration.

The six men gulped down a hasty breakfast of farina, the first cereal they had eaten in years, made with watered-down milk, and a slice of bread—real bread, made with rye instead of the mock bread of the camps.

Even though it was offered, they ate no butter. Zalmen was very firm about sticking to bland foods just now, as he had heard stories the night before while shouldering his way through the pandemonium of men and machines, soldiers and weapons. Some of the Flossenbürg survivors were dying in the fields after gorging on the candy bars and other food the soldiers had tossed in sympathy onto the roadside as they passed. Possibly their weakened systems couldn't digest that kind of food, and the vomiting, when they were already severely dehydrated, drained them of the final fluids needed for life. Maybe some were so close to dying that it was already too late to halt the trajectory. Possibly they fell victim to what later became known as refeeding syndrome, where severely malnourished people, upon eating a great deal of food, experience a burst of insulin that their bodies can't cope with, leading to cardiac failure—although that normally came days later, not hours.

Whatever the cause of the deaths, they had to be extremely careful, they decided.

The six men set off for Amberg, twenty miles away, where there was a convalescent hospital. Still exhausted from the previous days of marching, they tried to keep up one another's spirits, telling lies they all knew were lies, about the good things awaiting them. Sometimes they actually began to believe their own stories, and the mood grew almost giddy for a few minutes.

Not for Moshe, though. He had never known a blind man. He couldn't imagine how it would be possible to live on his own, earn money, find a woman willing to love him and have a family—if, after all the assaults on his body, he could even create children. He was young, better educated than most in that part of the world, multilingual, but he couldn't even tell day from night anymore. All he could do was cling to the desperate hope that doctors would be able to restore at least some sight in his right eye, the one that had offered a tiny strip of vision before the crack of light had closed.

Moshe said none of this. He simply walked, as they all did that day, until they could walk no more. They asked a farmer for bread and water as night fell, and sought permission to sleep not on his porch but in his barn. The farmer was a German, the enemy, and their regard for him was low. But decent people behave in a certain way, and now that they had had time to think about what probably had happened the night before in the farmhouse, they vowed never again to spread the lice and fleas that infested them in another stranger's home.

After days of walking past fields, farmhouses, and army equipment that had broken down or been abandoned at the side of the road, and nights spent sleeping in haylofts and scrounging for food, they finally reached Amberg, a city of about 40,000. It was April 29, not yet a full week since Allied forces had pushed through and staked their claim, and the town was in tortured disarray. Public transportation had stalled. Shopkeepers still hid their wares in case looters came through, or soldiers from one side or the other made declarations of ownership. A few survivors had arrived ahead of them and were roaming the streets and alleys with vacant expressions, sometimes erupting over small things.

The six presented themselves at city hall where record-keepers documented their survival. The brothers, like many survivors, decided to take different first names, less Polish-sounding. Yankel became Jack, Zalmen became Sigmund, and Moshe became Max. The new names signified new life, and also conferred separation from Poland, the country they despised now even more than they had in their younger years. The country of their ancestors and their youth had watched silently or participated as Jew after Jew was rounded up and taken away; as trains crammed with Jews lumbered past; as lines of ravaged, emaciated Jews in grimy uniforms marched past every morning to work; as crematoriums belched the ash of human bodies into the surrounding countryside. The Germans may have conceived the roundups and executions, but their Polish countrymen were complicit. They could never, even as old men, forgive that.

They received new clothes, a gift from the townspeople: underwear, socks, trousers, two shirts, shoes, and a jacket. Then they went to the public baths, where they submerged themselves in warm, glorious water. When they had scrubbed their bodies almost raw and wrapped themselves in crisp, new clothes, they set a match to their bug-infested uniforms and ruined shoes. They watched as the remnants of those years went up in flames—all but Max, who stood to the side and could only imagine how satisfying it would have been to see.

As Sigmund and Max entered the cool efficiency of the hospital, the odor of antiseptic hung sharp in the air, unexpected after all those years of living with the dull stench of filth and sickness. But it was not an unpleasant odor. It was the smell of promise.

In the exam room Max heard the horror in the nurses' voices as they pulled the hospital gown away from his bony chest and glanced at his thighs, no bigger than those of an eleven-year-old. He knew he looked awful, but he was impatient with their attentions. *The eye!* That's what they should be examining. Not the ruined eye, the hardened, calcified mass that seemed to interest them so much. The other one, he told the nurses, one after another. Examine that one. There had to be some process that would restore some of his sight.

He was not the first concentration camp survivor they had seen, but the numbers had not yet swelled to the level they eventually would, and they still marveled that men so malnourished, so frail, were still able to stand. They had no data about the long-term prospects and risks, but they knew Max's situation was dire. He weighed eighty-three pounds, they said. They feared his heart might suddenly fail or that other organs might, even now, shut down.

The first order of business, they said, was for him to gain forty or fifty pounds so he could build up his strength and reserves for the very real chance that he might get ill or require surgery.

"I don't care what I eat or if I eat at all," he snapped in frustration as day after day they forced food on him. "Every passing day is a wasted day. I need to be able to see again. This eye to be taken care of is what I need."

The nurses arranged an appointment with the one eye specialist in town, and Max awoke on that morning filled with apprehension. Maybe he would learn there was no hope of improvement. But the opposite was also possible, he reminded himself. He throbbed with anxiety, and when he reached the doctor's office he couldn't keep his breathing steady.

Dr. Hasselt silently examined and probed, first one eye and then the other. Max heard him push back his chair and place his instruments on the desk.

"Max, you will never see again."

The rage was instant. "That's *it*? *This* is what you tell me?"

He swung his head in the direction of the nurse who had brought him to the office. "What do you expect from a Nazi doctor?" Then again to the doctor: "And you—what are you a doctor for? You can fix nothing?"

The nurse walked him back to the hospital, and the director there, informed of the ophthalmologist's pronouncement, stopped by his room.

"Max," she said, "maybe we cannot tell everything now. Once you have gained some more weight, gained some strength, I will see that you get to Munich, to the university eye clinic."

He thanked her, but his mind was elsewhere, churning through thoughts unrelated to doctors and appointments. He had lived as a free man shackled by blindness long enough. He would kill himself. He might not be able to see, but he wasn't completely helpless. This he could do on his own. It required a great deal of thought, though.

How can I do it? he wondered. *I would jump into the lake to drown myself, but where's the lake? I can't find it. I could throw myself in front of a bus, but where's a bus?*

It wasn't easy for a blind man to kill himself. There was just one way, he decided.

Max told the nurse he was having trouble sleeping. She brought him a pill every evening, and he hoarded them, building a small pile in the bedside table, not sure how many he would need but assuming the task required a large handful. He didn't want to fail.

Maybe just three or four more days, he thought one morning, after a couple of weeks of caching pills. That afternoon a nurse discovered his stash. She took it away and gave him no more sleeping pills.

Another avenue closed—for now.

At the end of June, Max and Sig set off for the appointment with a Munich eye specialist, a hundred miles away. There was still not much public transportation available, and certainly nothing reliable, so the brothers received priority permission to travel on an army truck.

Sig paced while Dr. Meisner, the head of the eye clinic, examined Max. The doctor, they learned, had been a high-ranking Nazi officer, and this bothered them, but he was said to be among the very best. Dr. Meisner tilted Max's head back and sideways, pressed his fingers against the ridge of bone that bordered each eye. Max could hear the click of what he assumed was a small light turned on and off.

"Here is the circumstance we have, Max. Nothing could have been done to save the left eye, and now it must be removed and the eye cavity cleaned out. We will fit you with an artificial eye. As for the right eye, I don't know. If you had received treatment immediately after the injury, all or most of the sight could have been saved."

At this point, the doctor continued, it *might* be impossible to coax the right eye back to partial functionality.

Dr. Meisner performed surgery to remove the left eye and started Max on long-shot eye drops in an effort to revive the optic nerve. By late August, the surgery site had healed and the treatments on the other eye were complete.

"Take your brother home," Dr. Meisner told Sig. "Take care of him. Bring him back in December, and we'll see."

Home, Max knew from Sig, was three furnished rooms in Amberg that his brothers and friend Isaac had rented from a widow, Etta Eichenmueller, forced by finances to take in boarders. He imagined the small stuffy rooms where the three men would have to compress themselves to accommodate another person, a blind one. He would be nothing but a burden.

Max sat silent and still as Sig filled the journey with a steady stream of talk. Sig had come up with a way to earn enough money to keep them fed with a roof over their heads, he said. During the war, the routes and means by which Germans conducted commerce had faltered and then died. The ability to buy commodities had stagnated, so Sig and friends had set up a complex but very effective chain of bargain, barter, and trade.

There were interesting coffee shops in Amberg, Sig continued, where they could sip exotic coffee richer than anything Max could imagine, sweetened with as much sugar as they wanted. There were lively cabarets where the music was gay and the women very friendly. It was time, Sig figured, for the brother who had passed all of his adult years in camps or hospitals to venture into manhood.

Once they had arrived in Amberg, Max joined the others on their outings to taverns that reeked of cigarette smoke and stale beer, pressed forward by their energy. But he felt numb, distant. They didn't help, these outings.

During the days, while his brothers and Isaac worked, Max was installed in a straight-backed chair next to a window with nothing to do but listen to the birds and the noises from the street, people with real lives busily going about their business. He came to hate those sounds and those people. They should have been a tantalizing invitation to exploration, but they were nothing but a reminder of how incapable he was.

Mrs. Eichenmueller could see the desolation overtaking him, so in the afternoons, when her work was done, she sat and talked with him, read to him, told him of promising signs of change washing across Germany. Pitifully inadequate counterbalance, he thought, to the appalling truths seeping out about the horrors that had transpired during his years of captivity. And the full story wasn't even known yet, he figured.

In nearly two dozen countries, Jews had been rounded up and sent to one of the 20,000 labor camps or death camps Nazi Germany had established to imprison or kill Jews and other undesirables. About 90 percent of the Jews of Poland and Greece had been murdered; 75 percent in Yugoslavia; and at least a quarter to half in most of the rest of the countries that the Germans had occupied. This genocide—six million Jews, half of them Poles—in future decades came to be called the Holocaust. For now it was known as the *Shoah*, Hebrew for "calamity."

It was impossible to fathom so much evil, and when he tried to push this knowledge into some recess where it would haunt him less, he was unsuccessful. His mind filled with an ugly mass of swirling images.

His brothers and friends spent hours, night after night, discussing the military tribunals that would commence soon in Nuremberg, just forty miles from Flossenbürg, to prosecute the most prominent leaders of these systematic killings. But how could any trial possibly make up for the six million Jews and as many non-Jews—prisoners of war, Gypsies, the disabled, sympathizers, and others—who had been slaughtered?

To pull Max away from these thoughts, Mrs. Eichenmueller arranged for him to begin violin lessons with a blind music teacher named Mr. Pletschachesr, a man as kindly as he was talented. Max displayed no aptitude for strings, however, so Mr. Pletschachesr switched him to the accordion, which required less musical soul. Still nothing. The music teacher suggested that the hearing loss from having typhus might be contributing to Max's lack of musical ability, but both Max and his teacher knew that he simply had no talent for music. One more thing he couldn't do.

As the weeks passed Max's depression deepened. He could sometimes muster a slab of loathing toward his self-pity, but not very often, and not for very long. Most days, most hours of every day, he floundered in misery.

At night, wrenching nightmares about his time in the ghetto and the camps tormented him. His cousin Chayale, lifeless, blood pooled between her legs, the smeary broomstick used to rape and kill her flung aside. Scrawny men on their knees, naked, by the ditch, lips moving in prayer as each awaited the crack of the rifle placed against the base of their skull. The writhing man taking his final gurgling gasps while that massive German shepherd roared and ripped at his throat.

Max would awake drenched in sweat, heart racing, the fear as harsh as it had been when he'd first witnessed those horrors.

Sig learned that autumn of a brilliant eye doctor in Wiesbaden, 165 miles away. The brothers caught rides from truck drivers, hoping for a different outcome. The assessment remained the same.

In December, Max and Sig returned to the Munich eye clinic as directed, to see if the eye drops were accomplishing anything deep inside the remaining eye. Dr. Wesseli—who had headed the clinic before the Nazis had come to power and installed their own man—had replaced Dr. Meisner. A grandfatherly sort, he took his time examining Max, who, although not new to the facility, was new to him.

"The medicine did not work," Dr. Wesseli finally said. "I see no sign of improvement." He paused a moment before continuing. "I believe you should know this, too, so you can begin to live your life: In my opinion, no eye doctor anywhere will be able to do anything, unless—and I believe this is unlikely—someone in the future develops a completely new technique or therapy."

It was possible, the doctor knew, for a young man without a limb to live something close to a normal life; he had seen this often when farm and industrial accidents and wars stole arms and legs. Many men had also adjusted with relative ease to deafness. But complete blindness robbed a person of his sense of independence. Now that the final shred of hope had been snatched away, this man might decide to take his life, the doctor thought, not knowing that Max had already initiated the effort once before.

As Max began to rise, he felt a firm hand on his arm.

"You are going to be blind for the rest of your life," Dr. Wesseli said evenly. "What will you do about it? I see three options. Option one: Feel sorry for yourself, and be a burden to your brothers and to society for the rest of your life. Option two: The Nazis didn't kill you; now you can do it yourself. That will prove you are a coward. Option three: Try to restore your life."

He urged Max to enroll in a nearby rehabilitation school for blind adults. He would make a call to the superintendent to inquire whether Max could start with the next class.

"You will learn how to live independently. You will learn Braille and typewriting. You will learn a skill that will enable you to become self-supporting."

Trust a German to chart his life? Unlikely. Still, Max requested a few minutes to discuss the matter with Sig, who listened with interest.

"We have nothing to lose," Sig concluded.

Perhaps, Max told the doctor a few minutes later, he would be willing to try this idea of his. "And if it doesn't work, I can always return to option one or two."

On January 2, 1946, at the age of twenty-three, eight months after his liberation, Max began attending the Rehabilitation School for Blind Adults in Tegernsee, south of Munich, a residential school with an iron-fisted approach to transforming blind men into productive citizens. Seventy men arrived that snow-swept winter day, all former Nazis but Max. Dr. Wesseli had warned that would likely be the case.

"Don't let anything that anyone says or does bother you. Pay attention to your studies, learn as well and as fast as you can, and get out of there as quickly as possible."

Max's two roommates, Gerd Scholz and Sep Huber, had served as soldiers. Both had been conscripted to fight, however; they hadn't instantly raised their arms in support of Hitler and his policies and marched off to do his bidding. That mattered to Max. The three became good friends and had little to do with their other classmates.

The students learned, during the two to three years they would spend there, how to use knives and forks to eat food they couldn't see; how to shave themselves with a razor—tricky business, but a man couldn't walk about with nubs of stubble missed by imprecise swipes; how to take care of their clothes; how to walk from one place to another. They learned Braille. They learned how to avoid obstacles and keep themselves safe.

They were not coached on how to deal with the emotional aspects of having lost their sight. Raising the issue would have merely emphasized the disability, school officials thought, and they were devoted to banishing that sort of thinking, replacing it with a level of competence so high that graduates would entertain no feelings of weakness.

Classroom instruction took place from eight a.m. to four p.m., Monday through Friday, and from eight a.m. to noon on Saturday. Each night the men had hours of homework. The only breaks were two weeks of vacation every August and about ten days around Christmas. The grueling schedule was probably a deliberate strategy, Max thought, so as to allow no time for self-pity.

Vocational training offered instruction in professions that blind people could master and for which there was high demand: switchboard operators, court and medical transcriptionists, and physical therapists. Max chose physical therapy. He would not be a doctor, as his mother had hoped, but he would still be helping people. He found the study of anatomy and physiology mentally stimulating, and the practice sessions on veterans at a nearby hospital proved he was good at this work.

Every Saturday afternoon and Sunday young women from town volunteered to take a student or two to a movie or concert, for a walk, or to a cafe for coffee, and to read pages of their textbooks to them once they began studying for their vocations. School officials encouraged these interactions but warned the men against developing attachments, as becoming involved might interfere with their studies. There was undoubtedly another worry: that these men, still vulnerable because of their disability and most of them quite young, could be preyed upon by women motivated by the postwar shortage of males.

Helene, a few years older than Max, staked a regular claim on his weekends, taking him to cafes and reading his assignments to him. She worked at a jewelry store and had a son who didn't live with her. Max assumed that the child may have resulted from the kind of affairs of survival often conducted during war years, but he never asked, and she never offered.

It seemed casual enough for a time, but one Saturday when, after a concert, they stopped at a tavern for a beer, the air shifted sharply.

"It's too late to go back to the school now," Helene said. "Why don't you stay in my room tonight?"

Helene was well skilled in the ways of love, an enthusiastic teacher who helped Max imagine through his hands everything he couldn't see with his eyes. The affair didn't last long, however. Worried that he might neglect his studies if he divided his focus, Max put an end to it.

A few months later, in the summer of 1947, after he had been at the school for eighteen months, Max developed an eye infection and was admitted into the eye clinic in Munich for several days. There he met Hanka, a young patient in for a minor procedure. A kittenish girl with a sunny disposition, she, too, was a Holocaust survivor. It was the first time that Max had had the chance to develop a relationship with someone who might understand what made him feel so different, so unwilling to form attachments or reach out. He never expressed that to her, not wishing to taint their time together, but the fact that they shared an underpinning of similar trauma had significance, he thought, even if they didn't speak of it. They spent their time together out of view of the nuns who ran the facility, laughing about silly things and grabbing kisses like a couple of boarding school adolescents.

When his eye infection resolved and he returned to school, Hanka visited Max several times. Despite his vow to avoid entanglements, he found himself emotionally caught up with the young woman. She was lively and cheerful except for those occasional moments when a blanket of melancholy, heavy and impenetrable, would settle unexpectedly over her, and she had given every indication that she was ready to tackle life anew. For his part, Max had learned to be self-sufficient, was growing confident in his abilities, and he was making excellent progress toward being able to pursue a profession. Maybe a life with her was possible. Perhaps the next time she visited he would broach the idea of becoming serious.

He met Hanka's train the following Saturday, but before he'd had time to kiss her or say anything at all, she grasped one of his hands in both of hers and launched into what she had come to say. "I'm very fond of you, Max, but I can't ever marry you. I want a husband who can provide a good life—a family, a house, nice clothes. I was deprived of everything for a long time, and I realize now that I want what I want. You're blind and will never be able to provide me with any of those things. I'm sorry, but that's how I feel."

The words she spoke would have unmoored anyone on the brink of love, but they devastated Max. They confirmed that a blind man who allowed himself to get swept up in romantic thoughts about the future was engaging in folly. He studied harder.

In August 1948, Max graduated with a degree in physical therapy. He quickly passed the board exams, earned his license to practice and took a position the next month as a physical therapist at Bogenhausen Hospital in Munich. It had turned out exactly as Dr. Wesseli had promised, and Max allowed himself some pride in his accomplishment.

He and Sig rented a two-bedroom apartment on Dankwart Strasse in Munich. During the two and a half years that Max had been in school, Sig had opened a grocery store that was now being managed by his fiancée, Marianne. Brother Jack, meanwhile, had opened a tailor shop in Amberg and was engaged to marry a young woman named Violett.

The three brothers made regular visits back and forth between Amberg and Munich, the conversation always shifting at some point to the desire that each harbored to leave Germany, where their memories of the camps too often rose to the surface. Trying to atone for the devastation of the Shoah, the United Nations that year had carved the nation of Israel from the British Mandate of Palestine, and tens of thousands of Jews set their sights on a new life there. The Edelmans contemplated the same, the idea of helping to build that new state even more appealing now than it had been before the war.

Max no longer felt trapped or dependent on others. He could support himself with work that he enjoyed. He could take care of himself, and he could make his way around Munich on his own. He could not, however, unclench.

Dr. Wesseli, who had become as much a friend as a mentor, was concerned. He asked Max to dinner one crisp December evening, and when the meal was over and his wife had excused herself, Dr. Wesseli revealed what had prompted the invitation.

"You have come a long way since you were liberated. It's excellent, the progress you've made. Now, how do you intend to live with the scars of your ordeal? Go on being bitter, being angry, hating everybody for the evils done? What good would that do you? Negative emotions will consume you, Max. Don't hate. It's the acid that corrodes the soul."

It would take a dozen more years before the notion of "survivor guilt" began circulating among the medical community. It would take many more years beyond that before professionals would begin to discuss the similarities in Holocaust survivors that were so consistent—thick, periodically debilitating depression; nightmares; anger; disorientation and disassociation; attachment avoidance; strictly structured relationships—that survivor guilt received credence as a real disorder.

Not until decades later would symposia and papers describe the uniqueness of surviving a trauma of the magnitude of what had happened to the Jews—how the aftereffects appeared stronger and more encompassing the longer a person had been exposed; how most survivors feared that if they opened up, they would be met with reactions that minimized their experience, and so they shut down nearly all connection and feeling. Years into the future, experts would declare that when the fundamental balance of an entire people has been crossed out and overwritten with something so ugly and indelible, it has a profound and lasting impact that extends even to subsequent generations.

But on this December evening Max was just one of millions of Jews steeping silently in distress.

And Dr. Wesseli had encountered enough young men liberated from the camps to recognize the many anguished similarities among them. Some learned more quickly than others how to cope; some required a great deal of time to conquer it, or to prevent it from ruling their lives; some went to their graves, sometimes by their own hands, confused and angry.

Although Dr. Wesseli was heartened that Max's newly acquired self-sufficiency seemed to have made his depression less all-consuming than it had been before, he still worried that what remained was shot through with such bitterness—that it was so active and raw.

The doctor was right about the anger and about the need to extract himself from it, Max admitted that night. But if there was a passageway out, he didn't know how to find it.

"You could think about becoming an advocate for tolerance and respect for human life," Dr. Wesseli offered.

"There is value in that approach," Max acknowledged. He wasn't that strong, he told the doctor, but it was something he could try to live in small pieces.

"If you can be successful, it would be a lasting monument to your family," the doctor said.

There were no organized advocacy groups in Germany as far as Max knew. Most Germans he met, even those who were ashamed about what had taken place, didn't want to talk about those years, hoping to bury the whole period in the silence of history. Eventually, Max told himself, this ugly residue he was hauling around would dissipate, drifting into the atmosphere like a foul odor brought to nothing by a good, solid wind, and he would feel more normal again. He had to believe that.

Max began dating one of the hospital nurses, a well-built young woman with a big heart and infectious laugh named Lissy. Nearly every Saturday night they went to shows, often with Sig and Marianne, and later fell laughing into the little bed in her apartment, exploring each other with abandon, relishing their mutual passion. They took weekend trips to nearby resort towns and talked about everything from plays to politics, often into the middle of the night.

Soon they thought of themselves as a couple, although the label troubled Max. She was solid, and she was attached to Max, but he couldn't envision building a life with her. Her father had been a Nazi official, but that wasn't the issue.

"Maybe we just need each other," he said to Sig one evening. "Maybe we each need to feel a warm body, a body we care about. But I don't know if that is love. I only know that I like her very much."

Still, the couple talked of emigrating to Israel. Lissy was willing to convert, and she told Max often that she would be honored to be Jewish, to be his wife and live by his side in the new land. In the summer of 1950, they visited the Israeli representative in Munich, Dr. Sommerfeld, to discuss their thoughts. He didn't refuse them, but he offered no encouragement.

"The living conditions in Israel at this time are very hard, Max," Dr. Sommerfeld said. "You have already suffered a lot, and you should consider going to America or Canada. Save going to Israel for a later time, when things will be smoother and more settled."

Max had less than positive feelings about the United States, which had denied Jews entry in the buildup to the war, and which during the war had actively ignored what was happening to Jews and others in Europe. Although he was grateful the Americans had liberated him, too much had happened long before that. That's how Max saw it, and that's how all the survivors he knew saw it. However, Max's research indicated that no other country would take a blind Jew—not Canada, not Australia—so America became his focus, and that of his brothers.

Lissy's father's Nazi connections, however, barred her from entry.

"You know I can't stay here in Germany; it hurts too much. I have to go," Max told her as soon as he was certain what he intended to do.

She cried but did not beg. "You have to plan your life, and I cannot be an obstacle. That's what I am now, an obstacle."

Their time together had come to an end.

———

Not long after making this decision, Max traveled to Amberg to visit Jack and Violett. As usual, he made plans to see his former landlady, Mrs. Eichenmueller, and after they had finished their Sunday-afternoon dinner, a knock came at the door.

Mrs. Eichenmueller introduced Max to a young German woman named Barbara, the daughter of friends. The three made small talk, and Max liked the unhesitating way she answered his questions and asked her own. She sounded strong, competent, and caring.

"Let's go for a walk," Max suggested to her after they had talked for about an hour.

The two headed off to a cafe where he learned she was twenty-four, lived with her parents, was well-read, and worked as a secretary in an insurance office. He felt an immediate attraction.

They began to visit each other regularly, one or the other making the two-hour train ride between Munich and Amberg. They went to movies and concerts, dinners and cabarets. She was pleasant, generous with her affection, and not at all coy about checking into the hotel by the train station when she visited him.

Their fate as a dating couple, Max decided, lay in her hands.

"I don't have anything to make a decision about—either she takes me or she doesn't," Max told Sig one Sunday night after spending yet another weekend with her. "If I'm going to fall first, I could get very hurt. So I'm taking one step at a time. I can't afford being in love totally because it might come to an abrupt end."

Max willed himself to think little about the relationship when they were apart, but matters of the heart proceeded very fast during and after war. Barbara soon invited him to meet her parents, and Max realized she was becoming very serious.

He raised the idea of marriage not with a request for her hand or an invitation to a life together, but with a recitation of the future as he saw it. If she was going to continue with him, he wanted her to understand precisely what she would be getting into. First, they wouldn't stay in Germany; they would move to America. Second, the complications of his blindness must not be downplayed.

She didn't fear tackling a new continent, she said. Indeed, she found the prospect interesting, stimulating. The language barrier was unnerving, but many people had successfully inched their way into a new culture, and she saw no reason why they couldn't do the same. As for his blindness, she had considerable experience with disability, she reminded Max. Her father had been badly injured while serving during World War I, had a significant limp, was in pain much of the time, and couldn't hold a full-time job.

"I have lived all my life with a person who is disabled," she said. "I'm not a stranger to living with this."

"It's not all that simple—sighted people marrying blind spouses," Max countered. "Normal people have all their faculties. You can walk and talk and hear and see, and marrying somebody with a disability, it does not happen too often; it's not an easy decision. I won't try to convince you. The decision is for you to make, not me."

Those weren't the words of love a young woman longs to hear, but he wanted to be honest, and he wanted her to understand how hard life as the wife of a blind man would be. He would work to support her and whatever family they were able to establish, he told her. He would never be the sort of man who expected the wife to take on all of the domestic and child-rearing responsibilities. But, he added, "If you live with a sighted person you will have to do your share; if you live with a blind person, you'll have to do a share and a half. That's the way it is. At this moment, you may think we'll do just fine, but that's not reality. You must face it with open eyes. If you accept it, then maybe we'll make it, but otherwise, no."

"I understand your concerns, Max," she said. "I just don't share them." Now he knew where she stood.

At a lakeside resort that spring, he decided it was time to thrash out the details. "If we're going to get married," he said, "we have to do it soon. We have to start the process of immigration."

It would be an ordeal. They had to apply and go through many procedures with great speed. The American Congress had passed laws allowing an extra number of refugees and Holocaust survivors into America, but applications had to be made by June 30, 1951, two months away. Jack and Violett had already filed; Sig and Marianne hoped to do so, but they were waiting to see what Max would do.

Max and Barbara had additional complications. Barbara was German Catholic, and immigrants had to have sponsors to guarantee that the immigrant wouldn't need public assistance for at least two years. Since neither had relatives or friends in America to sponsor them, they had to rely on an organization to do the sponsoring. The Hebrew Immigration Aid Society sponsored Jews, while a Catholic organization sponsored Catholics. Getting two sponsoring groups to coordinate and meet deadlines was a prospect few wanted to count on if it was possible to avoid it.

She hadn't actually been proposed to in the way most women are, but Barbara knew Max well enough to realize these discussions were as close to some version of an invitation to share his life as she was likely to get. She agreed that they needed to take immediate action. She would, she told Max, convert to Judaism.

Max didn't ask her that night why she decided to marry him. In fact, he never, even in subsequent decades, put that question to her, regarding it a breach of privacy to ask. He accepted that once her mind was made up, she was at peace with her choice, and he should be as well.

They married at noon on May 5, 1951, at city hall in Munich. After the ceremony, they boarded a train for Amberg, where Jack and his wife hosted a newlyweds' dinner attended by Barbara's parents, sisters, and brothers, as well as the landlady-matchmaker, Mrs. Eichenmueller. The festivities were high-spirited but brief. The couple had to dash back to Munich to appear at the immigration office to fill out applications as a married couple.

Because the time for processing applications was so short, the chief rabbi excused Barbara from the usual conversion classes, but she had to go to the *mikveh* (ritual bath), where she stripped and submerged three times in the indoor pool. The rabbi signed the *ketubbah* (marriage contract), and Max and Barbara were officially a Jewish married couple.

Max had almost no attachment by then to the part of being Jewish that related to religion, but he considered himself a Jew by culture and heritage, and there was always the chance, he imagined, that they might move to Israel someday.

He continued working at the hospital, Barbara received a transfer to the Munich office of her insurance company, and the two awaited word of where they would be sent. They had no say about the city, since immigration officials believed that if everyone could declare a preference, all foreigners would descend upon New York City, snarling the systems there. Sponsoring groups existed in many cities, prepared to assist arriving Jews in certain numbers, so assignments depended on what those groups could handle at a given time.

The couple found it easy to settle into married life with each other, efficiently settling differences and respecting preferences, relishing the extra time they could spend at home with each other rather than on trains. But now that Barbara was spending every night in bed with Max, she realized that the nightmares she had witnessed during their courtship were as regular as they were severe. Nearly every night her husband awoke, panting, sweating, often screaming. He would get up, strip out of his drenched pajamas, wash, and return to her. Both of them would be restless and wakeful for the rest of the night.

While they were courting Max hadn't said much about the details of the nightmares that haunted him, and Barbara had been reluctant to press him to relive during his waking hours the things that poisoned his sleep.

Now she asked. He told her—but only very little. Hearing everything would sadden her too much, he thought. Also, he was sure that denying the images was the most effective way to move ahead and live life, so he kept most of it to himself.

In October of 1951, Sig and Marianne and Jack and Violett sailed for America—Jack assigned to New York, and Sig to Cleveland, a city Max had never heard of. Days later, Barbara and Max found that they, too, had been assigned to Cleveland.

In early December the couple boarded a military transport aircraft, the first time either had been on an airplane, with two suitcases and fifty-eight other people who had various disabilities. After refueling stops in Scotland, Iceland, and Newfoundland, they arrived two days later in New York City, to spend a week with Jack, acclimating to this new country—the odd cadence and strange sounds of this language they had to master, foods and spices so different they hardly seemed edible, and a dizzying wealth of goods and options.

Too few days later, Max and Barbara boarded a westbound train and the next morning, December 12, 1951, disembarked at Union Station in Cleveland.

A burly woman approached, confirmed in Yiddish their identities, escorted them to a taxi, thrust their suitcases into the trunk, and gave the driver the address and the fare. The couple slid into the back of the cab and weaved in and out of traffic, coming to a stop at a small apartment building on East 86th Street.

The woman who met them at the door introduced herself in passable German as Mrs. Foote, and presented the key to the apartment that they would be sharing with Sig and Marianne.

"Welcome to Cleveland," she said. "Sig and Marianne are coming home from work at five. Go ahead in and make yourselves comfortable."

The two-bedroom apartment was small, drafty, and musty; the furniture was old and wobbly; and they felt more than a little uncertainty. But it was a start.

Six

The Jewish organization that sponsored them paid the couple's rent for one month and provided $17.50 a week for bus fare to search for work and to buy food.

"I can't do anything about my eyesight, but I must learn this language very fast in order to be able to work," Max said that first night, when he and Sig reunited.

Barbara spoke no English either, but she could see, and she was strong. These were the only requirements for getting hired in one of the growing number of sweatshops cropping up in immigrant relocation cities to capitalize on the many people willing to do anything to earn five or six dollars a day.

She landed a job in a factory making ladies' coats, hard, nonstop work for seventy-five cents an hour. She returned home every evening with crops of blisters snaking through her fingers, bubbling burns from operating the steam machine to press the coats. Sometimes she cried while she sat at the kitchen table at night with her puffy hands in a bowl of ice to reduce the swelling enough so that she could move her fingers at work the next day.

"This will not go on for very long," Max said, trying to reassure her as a husband should, aching in his heart because it was probably not the truth. He couldn't put his hat on every morning and hit the streets like other men, searching for the right people and connections and half-open doors. That gnawed at his soul.

Once Barbara received her first paycheck, the sponsor's assistance stopped. That was as it should be, the couple believed: A person shouldn't rely on handouts. Still, it meant there was no chance of quitting no matter how bad her hands got, and what she earned was barely enough to get by.

Max had contacted the Cleveland Sight Center within days of arriving in the city, and he was assigned a Braille teacher so he could learn to read in English, a task he pursued with gusto. The couple went to night school on Mondays, Wednesdays, and Fridays to learn English together, and every Tuesday night they rode the bus to sit with a couple who'd arrived from Germany years earlier and who patiently conducted in English the kinds of conversations Americans all over the country were having. On Saturday mornings, a librarian for the Cleveland Library for the Blind spent an hour with the couple, doing the same.

Within five or six weeks, Max knew enough basic English to make himself understood and to understand much of what others were saying. But continuing his career in physical therapy, he had learned, was out of the question for now. The United States had no reciprocity agreement in the allied medical professions with Germany, so Max would have to return to school for a year or more, then pass the state board exam. His English, though improving rapidly, wouldn't be good enough to manage that for many months to come. He couldn't allow Barbara to continue as sole breadwinner for the time it would take to earn his license.

An ad in the daily newspaper for a health club masseur drew Barbara's attention one afternoon, and Max applied. Therapeutic massage had been part of his training in Germany; in fact, he was overqualified for this job, but if he could get hired, it could serve as a stepping-stone. Even if it didn't lead to something better, they needed the money, and it was something he could do well even with less-than-perfect English.

The health club manager had very few questions for Max when he arrived for the interview. A brisk woman with a tinny voice and an air of impatience swirling about her, she conducted their conversation with what seemed like something beyond haste, maybe abruptness. As this was his first interview in his new country, he wasn't quite sure how to read it.

Maybe this is how people in America behave, he thought. She rustled some papers on her desk and declared that another person was applying for the job and that Max should not call her again. She would contact him with her decision.

As Max was leaving her office, she passed him something that felt like a folded piece of paper. Probably additional information about the job or the expectations, he figured.

"What is this?" he asked when he found Barbara, who had accompanied him on the several buses required to get there.

"A five-dollar bill."

Max, furious, stormed back into the office. "I did not come here for charity but to apply for a job," he snarled. He could not, in his anger, come up with all the right words in English, so he spoke some in German. He was sure she caught his meaning, however, when he slammed the money on her desk and stomped out of her office.

⁓

The Jewish Family Service Association arranged soon after the job-interview unpleasantness for Max to meet Lee Feldman, a counselor at the State Bureau of Vocational and Rehabilitation Services for the Blind. A visually impaired veteran of World War II, Feldman knew what kind of roadblocks would confront a blind man trying to find work, and told Max that if he was willing to undergo four or five months of instruction, he might be able to get hired as an X-ray darkroom technician.

It would be isolating work, consisting of nothing more challenging than following the same routine hour after hour, day after day, almost like being on an assembly line. But there was a demand for such technicians, he said, and Max's obvious appreciation for structure made this a good prospect for him because it involved following prescribed steps, carefully timing everything, and moving quickly when the buzzer signaled it was time to slide the film from one tray to the next.

To prepare, Max would have to learn how to use a white cane, something he hadn't learned since the Germans took a different approach to mobility training. And he would have to memorize bus lines and schedules so he could get to and from training and then the job, which might—depending on which hospital hired him (*if* one hired him)—be a long distance from his apartment.

Max was eager, he assured Feldman, to do whatever was necessary.

His mobility training began immediately.

The instructor, a blind chain-smoker named Jim, had a gravelly voice and a no-excuses approach to life. "When you walk down the street," Jim said on their first day together, "and you bump into a pole and get a bloody nose, you have two options: Go back home, clean up, and start over again, or continue going wherever you have to go and clean up there. Big boys don't cry."

The two got on well.

Max began his technician training barely two months after arriving in the United States—nervous because his English was still halting, and also because he wasn't sure how the techs in the hospital who were to teach him would react to having a blind man thrust into their operation. But the employees were friendly and patient and devoted themselves to helping him succeed. They spent their lunch hours encouraging him through conversations to help spur his English along, and one, thinking music might help (not realizing until it was too late that Max was tone-deaf), taught him the popular Irving Berlin song, "Blue Skies."

When Max completed training four months later, Feldman reported that he'd found him a darkroom technician position at the Cleveland Clinic. The pay would be one dollar an hour, and Max would be on probation for six months rather than the customary ninety days, because there was discomfort among some at the hospital about his ability to do the job. Max accepted the job and the terms.

Feldman arrived at Max's apartment soon after sunrise on October 20, 1952, to accompany him on the bus for his first day at work.

"There's something you must remember," Feldman said as they bumped along the streets, shouting above the roar of the shifting gears, "and that is that you'll have to work harder than your sighted coworker. You'll have to be more loyal than your sighted coworker. Never be late for work if there's any way at all to avoid that, and don't leave at quitting time unless you've finished what you're in the process of doing. If you practice those things, your boss will say you're a good employee. He will never say you're an excellent one, but you'll have a job. This is how things are."

Art, the first darkroom coworker Max met, a tall man with a sharp, chafing voice like a rag being ripped, immediately made it clear that Max's presence displeased him. He didn't like Jews, he said, and suggested that no one else in the department did either. Then he turned his back and said no more. Others were slightly more hospitable.

Workers had thirty minutes for lunch; Art took an hour or more every day. Max responded by eating lunch at his desk while continuing to process X-rays. Eventually Art was fired, replaced with a visually impaired employee, and, a couple of years after that, a blind one.

"The job is not one that I like or that I really wanted," Max told Jack in a letter he typed soon after starting work at the clinic. "But at least I can work and not live only off the earnings of my wife. And when a physical therapy job becomes available, I can apply for it. I am permitted to work as a physical therapist if it's under the supervision of a licensed therapist. Or, as an alternative, once my English is strong, I can take courses to become licensed in this country."

Barbara's English improved rapidly as the months passed, largely because she was a voracious reader who devoured best-sellers and romance novels while riding buses or sitting in the living room at night, listening to the radio, a fat dictionary at her side. This helped her to secure a new job, making parts on an assembly line for twice the salary. A few months later, she shifted to an even better job in the miniature lamp division at the General Electric plant.

The couple celebrated their first Thanksgiving in America by walking two miles through holiday-quiet neighborhood streets to the Miami Deli and ordering their first American-style turkey dinner. Less than a year had passed since their arrival, and they had ascended sufficiently that they felt it was safe to rent a slightly bigger place, buy furniture, and make Cleveland their permanent home.

Wherever they moved, they knew, it had to be on the bus line so each could get to work every day, and Barbara scoured the newspapers with a city map and bus route map in hand. Spotting an ad for half a duplex they could afford, she called to inquire. The owner asked if the couple was "safe." She wasn't sure she understood the question or the meaning of the word, she said. He wasn't opposed to immigrants, which, he could tell by her accent, she was, he responded; he just wanted to be sure they were Christians.

"No," Barbara said. "We're Jewish."

"No apartment."

The classified-ads search continued, circles in black blooming over columns of gray. The couple visited a large apartment building that sounded especially promising.

"They don't rent to the blind," the manager declared when the Edelmans presented themselves.

When, days later, Barbara saw an ad for another apartment that seemed worth considering, she climbed on the bus and went alone. She inspected the place, signed the lease, and handed over the checks for the rent and security deposit, mentioning that she had a husband but offering no additional information. If anyone there had an issue with the blindness or Jewishness of the man who arrived with her a few days later, it was never mentioned.

The couple bought cheap furniture, piece by piece, never more than they could afford; some black metal fans to churn the swampy air, so hot and still in the city during the long summer months; and a sewing machine from Sears & Roebuck so Barbara could make dresses for work.

By now they had a few friends, and some knew about Max's background as a physical therapist. One and then another asked for therapeutic massage, or referred friends to him. Soon he had five regular customers he treated after work or on the weekends, a welcome boost to their income and to his morale.

Max had always found learning new languages easy, and he endeavored to ferret out and master every idiosyncrasy and nuance of this perplexing English language, crammed with verbs with past tenses that break convention, confounding words that sound the same but have different meanings, and contractions that don't make sense. He listened to the radio, voices of Americans he couldn't envision, perpetual background noise he monitored carefully, remembering all the new words, asking Barbara to look them up in the dictionary if his Braille dictionary wasn't nearby. He decided NBC's Edwin Newman and CBS's Edward R. Murrow were America's finest speakers, storytellers, and linguists, and he stopped whatever he was doing whenever their voices spilled from the wooden box, appreciating the rhythm and cadence and wealth of words that painted such vivid pictures. Maybe regular exposure to them would infuse the language part of his brain with a richness that reading and studying alone did not accomplish, he thought.

He also made a request of the friendlier doctors, nurses, and staff people at work.

"Please. If I ever make a mistake when I am talking, if I use the wrong word or the wrong inflection, I want you to tell me. I will not be offended. The only way I can learn is if I am corrected."

In time he developed a vocabulary that far surpassed those of many people born and raised in this country, though he never lost his heavy accent or his distinctive flat delivery common to those who grew up in Eastern Europe.

In 1954, a physical therapy position became available at another hospital. Because the employee would be working under a physical therapist, a license wasn't required, and Max scheduled an interview. As he sat with the personnel director, who reviewed his résumé and documents, he discussed some of his more challenging cases in Germany, and she declared him well qualified.

"I don't make the hiring decisions, Mr. Edelman; the department supervisor does. I'd like to call her in now and have her speak with you."

Max was feeling optimistic. There hadn't been the slightest hint of misunderstanding or miscommunication. The woman seemed impressed with his training and his knowledge.

He heard the door open. *The supervisor,* he thought. Silence filled the office, trussed with a queer, heavy tension. He heard the personnel director start to introduce him, but before a full sentence had left her lips, the supervisor spoke.

"He's blind. I don't want a blind person, " she said, her tone sharp, almost angry. She slammed the door as she left.

Max grabbed his cane, said good-bye to the personnel woman, who was sputtering apologies, and made his way to the waiting room to collect Barbara, who, like Max, had taken a vacation day to come to this interview.

"I have not been so humiliated since the concentration camp," he growled. "I wish I had the money to go back to Germany."

Max had expected and had tried to gird himself for the fact that some people would dismiss him—some would even pity him because they knew he couldn't see. What he hadn't expected was the level of animosity he was encountering because of his blindness. For his Jewishness, yes, he had dealt with that since childhood, but not for his blindness.

He began to regret his decision to come to America. At least in Germany he'd had a career he enjoyed, one that brought satisfaction and respect, and whatever struggles he'd had with being blind were internal, not the result of nastiness from others.

He sank into a crater of gloom—dangerous, he knew, because experience had taught him that once the negative feelings gained entry, the memories and the hostility he felt about the war surged forth with special ferocity. It happened that day; it happened many times in subsequent years.

The nightmares, too, had journeyed across the Atlantic with him like a dark, determined shadow, and they worked him over with the same intensity they had in Germany. He lived something close to a double life: working husband during the day, and at night, when he slept, a dead-legged captive, unable to escape the horrors of the camps. It seemed especially unjust that although blackness was all he saw during the day, when he dreamed, everything appeared in full, awful color: crimson blood gushing from a skull blasted open by a single rifle shot; the blazing blue eyes of the guards who had beaten him until he could no longer see their eyes; the sharp, blood-stained muzzle of a big German shepherd diving deeper into the mangled neck of a screaming man.

When he was able to thrash himself awake—heart slamming against this ribs like a frantic animal—it was a very long time before he could breathe normally again. After especially bad, battering nights, when Barbara couldn't soothe him, he would arrive at work, tattered and drained. Forget it, he lectured himself as he moved film from tray to tray. Move on. His tactic for achieving this was to cram the past into a vault he never accessed, at least during the day, when he could force his mind to follow the precise routines necessary to earn his pay. In the mean hours of the moon, though, when he was loose and vulnerable, the ugliness oozed out, leaving him chafed and angry. He despised his inability after all this time to be stronger than the memories and images, the anger and the emptiness.

"It was not enough that they almost killed me, that they left me blind," he said to Barbara one morning. "Their genius is that they make those of us who lived through it nearly die again every day."

No one at work knew anything about his background, nor did most of his friends. His watch and shirtsleeve usually covered the KL tattoo riding just above his left wrist. He did not purposefully hide his past, but he had no interest in sharing it, never inviting questions or dropping hints. Admitting to that kind of pain only makes others uncomfortable, he believed, and acknowledging misery begets greater misery. That was how his parents had lived, never wallowing in unpleasantness or distress. Sig and Jack, who had suffered many of the same miseries, took much the same approach, rarely speaking of the war years, trying, Max assumed, to tamp out the anguish and pain just as he was.

Others, too, had nourished his disinclination to speak of the past. When Max had started at the clinic, his job coach, Feldman, always quick with advice, had offered some on this score as well. "No one is interested in your experiences, and no one cares how and where you were blinded," he said. "If you are asked, say as little as you possibly can."

Max's standard answer, when someone asked how he had lost his sight, was: "During the war."

The couple carved out their place as hardworking immigrants with boundless drive to learn and achieve, and, as their life became less threadbare, allowed themselves some diversions. They went to movie matinees; they joined Sig and Marianne on a road trip to New York to visit Jack and Violett, strolling Fifth Avenue and Times Square and eating in old Jewish delis; they spent every Sunday afternoon with a small circle of friends. They celebrated Hanukkah and Yom Kippur, usually with Sig and his wife, and they also celebrated Christmas—in the way Barbara had in her youth. She decorated the apartment, made holiday cookies and the special Christmas bread known as *stollen*, and knitted gifts for everyone she knew.

Four years after they arrived in Cleveland, they discovered, to their amazement, that a baby was on the way. Barbara had been told in Germany that she was unlikely to ever be able to bear a child, and they could hardly believe their good fortune. Their little apartment wouldn't do, so they found a third-floor, two-bedroom apartment in a predominantly Jewish neighborhood, intending to raise the child Jewish and engage him or her in religious study. Barbara set about preparing a bedroom for the infant, making curtains and buying furniture. They didn't know if they would have a son or daughter, and they didn't care.

The crib had been set up and the diapers stacked on a changing table when, after supper on February 24, 1955, Barbara cleared the table, washed the dishes, and told Max it was time to go to the hospital. Sig arrived to drive them and stayed in the waiting room with Max until 3:30 the next morning, when a door opened at the end of the corridor.

"*Mazel tov!* You have a son!" announced Dr. Abrams, placing the six-pound, eight-ounce infant into Max's arms.

Sig grabbed his Kodak and snapped pictures.

Max, having learned the custom of such things, stopped at the drug-store on his way to work to buy IT's A BOY cigars for the men and candies for the women.

Barbara left the assembly line to raise the baby they named Stephen. Although this put a significant crimp in their finances, it was important, they agreed, for a child to be raised by his mother, in the early years at least. Cutting back on movies and weekend lunches out and mending clothes instead of buying new ones were not unacceptable sacrifices.

They did indulge in one modest luxury. Barbara took driving lessons, passed the test, and they bought their first car, a used blue Chevrolet, so she would no longer have to balance grocery bags against her chest while pushing Steve's stroller home from the market.

Max continued his relentless pursuit of English language mastery; he and Barbara studied for and passed the citizenship test to become natural-ized citizens of this new country; and they reveled in being parents, rarely going anywhere or doing anything if toddler Steve couldn't join them.

A second robust son, Richard, arrived four years later. To accommodate the larger family and growing boys, during the following years they moved to slightly bigger, slightly better apartments, Barbara continuing to be a stay-at-home mother, baking, reading to her sons, and taking them to museums. When Steve was in third grade and Rich was nearly four, they enrolled their youngest in a preschool program so that Barbara could return to GE to ensure there would be enough money for college.

Barbara left for work each morning at seven, and Max got the boys fed and out the door in time for school and preschool, then dashed off to his own job, still sliding film through trays five days a week. When Max arrived at the bus stop after work each evening, Steve was always waiting—rain, snow, or broiling summer heat—to walk his dad home.

As with his parents before him, Max was strict. It was his job to make sure his sons appreciated the value of perseverance and self-respect, that they understood integrity is essential for living an honorable life, and that no one should do less than capability and circumstance allow. The boys learned at a very young age that their father appreciated punctuality and predictability, demanded politeness and reliability, had no patience for laziness or underperformance, and would not tolerate excuse-making. As and Bs on report cards were acceptable; Cs were not.

"If you're capable of doing better, you should," Max said with regularity, and "If you don't learn something new this day, it's a wasted day."

These were the things a father does to help turn a boy into a man, and Max was without equal in attending to that. Barbara, quick with a hug and a pan of German plum cake when an achievement or a disappointment warranted it, could supply the gentleness and understanding that Max's mother had given her children.

They had their comforts and their routines. Game nights with Scrabble tiles in Braille and dominoes, everyone a fierce competitor. The special seven-layer cake for every birthday. Dinner at 6:30 every evening, always from scratch—brisket, roasted chicken, gingerbread—which Barbara put together from memory or instinct, never from a recipe.

Barbara and Max built every piece of their life around nurturing their sons into full bloom. The couple finally joined a congregation so the boys could go to Jewish summer camp every year and could, when the time came, begin religious training so they would have a foundation of faith that they could choose to embrace or reject in adulthood.

Every summer, all four packed up the family car, a bag stuffed with sandwiches nestled in the backseat between the boys, and they hit the highway, rolled-down windows admitting a blast of wind that swept papers and wrappings around like crazed birds. They went to New York sometimes, where they visited the Statue of Liberty and the United Nations building, and rode the elevator to the top of the Empire State Building. Both boys developed keen observation skills, describing for their dad the big and tiny pieces of what they were seeing so perfectly that he could picture in his mind things he had never actually witnessed—buildings that soared so high that their tops were lost in the wispy fog of a rainy day, sidewalk grates bigger than tabletops that belched forth the mysterious sounds of the netherworld of tunnels, pigeons so street-savvy that they fluttered within inches of fast-moving feet to pluck up crumbs and crusts.

Washington, D.C., was the destination one summer, so the boys could experience their country's seat of power. And to give their city-boy sons a taste of something different, they spent a week at a farm in Pennsylvania, where they swam in a pond, went on hayrides, and watched cows being milked.

"It's a good life we've made, Max," Barbara said after one of those trips, and Max agreed.

As the boys grew older—Steve, driven and goal-oriented, Rich, playful and easygoing—each with his own talents and interests, each with his own approach to school and the religious training their parents insisted upon, Max felt increasingly inadequate. They needed things now that he couldn't provide.

Steve had become quite a baseball player and dreamed of playing third base for the Cleveland Indians. Max wished he could practice with him, chuck balls at him in the park, watch games with him on TV. That he couldn't made Max feel he wasn't fully doing his job as a father. He attended his son's Little League games, he and Barbara off to the side, she telling Max when Steve was up at bat, describing his swings and his progress around the bases. They went to Cleveland Indians games sometimes, and Max and the boys spent long summer afternoons by the radio, listening to major league games, cheering and groaning.

Rich loved fishing. How wonderful it would have been, Max thought gloomily, if on a weekend he could have loaded his son into the car and driven to a lake, instructed him in the mysteries of flies and ripples in the water. In 1970, when Rich was eleven, they rented a summer cottage near a pond stocked with bluegill. Father sat next to son on the bank, Max weaving the worms onto the hooks, Rich doing the fishing, having taught himself the finer points of casting and reeling.

Max's bouts of depression never diminished, arriving and staying by their own clock and course. He never missed work, even when he was utterly disconsolate and disoriented, muscling his way through the hours by disconnecting himself from any thought but the task at hand.

This same distancing from emotion was also asserting itself more often at home. It might be difficult for his family to witness, he supposed, but it kept him from being completely swamped and unable to function.

One of his most treasured friends was a Polish immigrant with whom he and Sig spent nearly every Sunday afternoon, drinking coffee and arguing about current events. Michael Lewinow had been a psychologist in Poland, and though he never practiced in the United States (because he couldn't, despite enormous effort, master English sufficiently well), his knowledge was broad. An amusing sort with a great gift for gab, Lewinow sometimes shared his observations about the probable or suspected emotional and mental health of people in the news. He always seemed to be right on the mark, his friends agreed.

One afternoon, after Sig had left the room, Lewinow leaned forward in his chair and began speaking to Max in Polish, his voice soft but serious. "Max, you're my friend, and I must tell you this: I'm concerned. I've known you long enough to know that you're sabotaging your own life. You're denying an important reality, Max. You are blind, and you're angry about it. People see a distant, angry man closed into himself, and they think you're angry at them. The way you present yourself keeps you even more removed than you purposefully make yourself. You need to snap out of it."

Max was furious. He hadn't invited this kind of intimacy, and he felt attacked. It was the truth as Lewinow saw it, and Max believed in truthtelling, but the man had no right to break the unwritten rules of friendship. Max said none of this that afternoon, or ever. He fumed silently, and their friendship cooled. Although they still got together nearly every Sunday, Max pulled back, a fortress against further uninvited incursions.

He was middle-aged now, and there was, Max thought, little likelihood of changing much about himself. He wasn't sure how to go about making any changes; in any event, he wasn't sure he wanted to—wasn't even sure that every unpleasantness he encountered could or should be laid directly at his own feet. Years later, when he began to experience something of a lightening of spirit, he wished he had given his friend's analysis serious consideration at the time it was presented—a priceless gift, even though it felt like a harsh rebuke.

"I allowed myself to be too preoccupied with the things I couldn't do because of my blindness rather than to focus on the things I could do, and do well," he confided in a letter years later.

But at that moment, he could only move forward in the ways he always had, which had brought him this far. He wouldn't risk a misstep that might jeopardize everything he had built. He had to keep working at his job so there would be money for his sons' college educations, and he had to continue to reject the hope of someday resuming a full career in physical therapy, rather than just dabbling on the side. He had to invest most of his energy into staying in control so that the nightmares and the depression wouldn't completely absorb him, so that emotion wouldn't carry him to a place from which he might not be able to return. A man can only do so much at once.

He did, however, pursue new learning. He took a correspondence course, offered by the Hadley School for the Blind in Chicago, in Hebrew Braille. That class didn't really lie outside his ken, but another did. He signed up for an adult education class in upholstering.

The instructor, Mr. Chenissi, was stunned when Max tapped his cane into the classroom and took a seat. The teacher went about his introductions and detailed his plans for the weeks ahead: a chair seat first, then a full chair or sofa, eyeing the blind man, composed and still.

"I don't know about this," the teacher said to Max after class. "I don't believe it's possible for a blind person to do this correctly."

"Give me a chance, please," Max responded. "I don't know if this will work either. Maybe I will fail, but I will try very hard. And neither of us will have lost much if I do not succeed."

Max proved to be the best of students, requiring help from a sighted person, it turned out, only for cutting the fabric and stitching the piping, assistance Barbara provided. In all other ways, his hypersensitive fingers—so capable after years of doing the work his eyes did not—felt out and followed the tiniest channels, locating angles and drop-offs like a sculptor pressing the formless into something of beauty.

One evening, Rich joined his father in the basement work area, where Max was re-covering the cheap sofa and chairs they'd purchased years earlier, battered from the activities of two lively boys. After a while Rich grew quiet.

"Unc couldn't make a couch like that, could he?" the boy said at last, referring to his uncle Chris, Barbara's brother, who had immigrated to America. He was a competent fixer-upper who always had a home-improvement project going on in his own home.

Max couldn't, for a few seconds, force words past the clot of sadness in his throat.

"No one can do everything, of course. But, no, Unc couldn't make a couch like we do."

This simple question from a ten-year-old proved, he figured, that a boy needed to find something, just one thing, that would allow him to be proud of his dad.

Max was sure his sons had suffered more than they said from having him as their father, in ways sighted people would never imagine.

When Steve was in eighth grade, his school held a father-son evening where retired Cleveland Browns offensive tackle and placekicker Lou Groza was the guest speaker. People mingled and chatted with one another and the teachers as Max sat alone, marooned in his chair, trapped by his inability to make his way through the crowd. Only one person approached: the father of Steve's best friend. Max regarded the behavior of all the rest as simple avoidance of a blind person, which he had experienced many times before.

"I felt ashamed and sorry for Steve," he told Barbara that night in bed. "He couldn't have helped but notice it, even though he might be too young to understand it completely."

Barbara suggested this might be the time for the two of them to talk with the boys about the blindness. Max didn't respond. He had folded into himself again, brooding. She recognized this posture. It might be a day or more before he would emerge and reconnect in his somewhat remote but normal-for-him way.

Max didn't speak then with Steve or Rich about the social difficulties related to his blindness, believing that burdening them with a father's troubles would be selfish.

He also never mentioned his Holocaust experiences.

Max and Barbara entered a period, a long, several-month period, of serious marital unhappiness, the arrival of which, after twenty years together, brought as much mystification as pain. No shouting matches erupted, no sharp exchanges or slamming doors. They were both too restrained for that. Also, there really wasn't a single issue or problem to fight through and get beyond, they both knew. More, it seemed, there had been a gradual awareness of disappointments and discomforts, of diverging thoughts about how things should be, an accumulation of little things grown too big to ignore.

But although the apartment grew silent and tense, there was no talk of divorce. Their sons were not yet through school, and they agreed that since having a family had been a mutual decision, they would honor that and raise their sons together, in a two-parent home.

Eventually time, events, and the obligation to family lessened the misery. Things were never again precisely as they had been, but there was never again talk of unhappiness.

Their routines continued, and the years flowed on with typical bumps and joys. Serious-minded Steve graduated in the top 10 percent of his high school class and chose to attend Washington University in St. Louis on a full scholarship. Rich, still in high school, now the only son at home, became the one to begin to unlock the family secret.

Both boys knew their father had been "blinded in the war," knowledge they had gained more from osmosis than through direct conversation. But as they reached their teens they noticed that many of the Braille library books Max always had stacked up were about the war and the Holocaust. There was also that tattoo, which they never asked about because they sensed they weren't supposed to. They were smart boys, though, and they had drawn conclusions.

Rich finally broached it directly. He was studying the Holocaust in school, he said to his father. He had to write a paper, and he wondered if Max would be willing to help.

It was impossible for Max, of all people, with his dedication to education, to deny a request like that, Rich knew. And in this way, the younger son began to learn a little about how the Holocaust had impacted his father.

"I had no choice," Max told Sig later. "I wanted him to get a good grade. I gave him a broad stroke of the brush, not a lot of details."

The crack was narrow, but his son hauled out information a little at a time.

"I owe it to him," he said to Barbara one night. "His classmates, kids whose parents are not survivors, should not know more about that time than my son does."

Rich finished high school and set off to college, eventually studying law enforcement, though it took him some time and a transfer before he settled on his major. Steve got a job as an accountant and lost his young wife to lymphoma. Each of Max's sons were trying to find their footing in difficult times, and Max kept his distance, not trusting himself to handle the conversations well, or appropriately.

"I never enjoyed the confidence of either one of my sons. We didn't develop the openness, closeness, and trust required. That is no doubt my fault," he said in a letter to his grandchildren years later. He regretted it—but couldn't explain why or fix it.

Remarkably healthy physically, given what his body had been through, Max suddenly began having sharp stomach cramps resistant to every effort he made to quell them. He made an appointment with his doctor.

It was colon cancer.

The day before his surgery, Max gave Sig money to buy two cemetery plots.

"My will is in order, and when you take care of this I will be at ease. Whatever will be, will be."

The surgery, performed the day after Thanksgiving, 1983, was successful, if not minor. Max bounced back with surprising speed for a man of sixty. In the new year, he went back to work.

During his weeks of recuperation, he had given serious thought to suggestions made regularly by a few people who knew something about his background, suggestions he had always rejected. Maybe it was time, he now thought, to do as they had recommended—to share some of his experiences. He wasn't ready to talk yet about his years in the camps, but maybe he could put some of it on paper as his old friend, Jacob Freid, editor of the *Jewish Braille Review,* had urged. Silence and the isolation Max had constructed for himself could no longer be an option, Freid had insisted. The few survivors still alive had an obligation to tell their stories.

"If I ever intend to do it," Max told Sig, the first person with whom he shared this idea, "now is the time. If the surgery told me anything, it's that it is much later than I thought."

"It will be hard on you. Hard on Barbara and the boys."

"Yes. It will."

Max told Barbara that he intended to write a piece, that he thought it would be easier to write than speak it. "In this way, maybe I will be able to pull the cork. I don't know."

He wasn't sure the cork should be pulled, but he was no longer certain it shouldn't be.

He typed and Barbara read, correcting his spelling from time to time. He described incidents she had never been aware of, and she stopped sometimes to ask him about them, and often, to do research on her own.

What emerged, much later, was a ten-page manuscript he called "Liberation Day of a Blind Survivor." It wasn't everything he had endured—far from it. He wasn't ready for that. It was a few details in a competent if remote style. He sent it to Freid with a note saying: "Do with it whatever you please."

Fried called to say he would publish it and suggested Max submit a copy to other publications. In time it appeared in the *Cleveland Jewish News,* the *Plain Dealer,* and the *News Herald.*

In 1988 the American Council for the Blind named it the year's best submission and sent a plaque, which Max hung over the desk where he typed, and a check for $200. Two months later, at the ACB convention in Columbus, Max presented that check, plus $200 he and Barbara had donated and a $100 contribution from a friend to serve as seed money for a scholarship fund for blind students. Once presented with the idea and the money, the state group launched its first-ever scholarship fund solicitation effort, an endeavor so successful that they awarded a scholarship to a blind student every year after. The board of directors voted to call it the Max Edelman Scholarship Fund.

Seven

Soon after New Year's Day in 1990—after thirty-seven years, three months, and one week of sliding films from one tray to another—Max retired from the Cleveland Clinic. Technology was advancing and encroaching so rapidly, he knew he would be called sometime soon into an office to hear that his job was being eliminated.

"I want to be the one who decides when I won't be working anymore," he told Barbara, "not have someone else decide that for me."

He arrived at the hospital that final day, pressed and polished, creases sharp in his trousers, as always, knowing there would be a cake-and-punch send-off. What he hadn't expected was the throng of doctors and nurses and aides and other personnel who made their way through the long corridors to pay homage to his decades of unfailing precision and reliability. For hours he stood, straight and formal, shaking hands and receiving good wishes.

Days later, he took the first step toward constructing the kind of active retirement he knew he needed. He applied for a guide dog.

Over the years, many people had suggested he get a guide dog to expand his freedoms. His boss wouldn't permit a dog in the darkroom, so pursuing it was pointless, he told the advice-givers, one after another. Max did not mention the much greater issue: that all dogs, no matter the size, no matter if on leashes or not, terrified him. A dog didn't have to bark or growl; it didn't even have to approach. Just the jingle of a collar and tag a few feet away or the sound of a dog snorfling in the dust along a fence line brought fear sweat instantly to the surface, made his stomach drop and his heart race. He couldn't breathe well or think clearly until he had moved a safe distance away.

Max had tried to convince himself that although it might be understandable that this fear had bored into him like an awl, in his present circumstances it was not only ridiculous, it was excessive, life-limiting, and pathological. He had read enough to know all the terminology. He had not, however, located any meaningful advice for overcoming it.

Still, he was determined to have a guide dog. He would no longer be spending ten hours every weekday working in the hospital or traveling to or from it, so he would have a great deal of free time, and he didn't want to spend it cloistered.

"They don't let blind guys drive," he said to Sig, "or I would get where I need to be on my own."

Barbara's arthritis—in her ankles, feet, and hands—had become so severe in recent years that getting around was difficult for her, especially when it was cold or damp. When her mobility was limited, so was Max's. It would be excruciating, he knew, if the hours of his retirement were dictated by the schedules, availability, or interests of others.

"That is not a life for me."

A guide dog, then. That was the answer.

He and Barbara discussed Max's fear before submitting the application, the changes to their lives that would come from having a dog. Not just an ordinary dog like other people had, but one that would always be with them, sleeping in their bedroom, going to restaurants and their sons' homes, one that would require daily walks and attention. It would change everything.

Barbara understood better than anyone Max's consuming need to go where and when he wanted, not to feel trapped. "I think we have to do this," she told her husband. "I don't know how to live with a dog, but I suppose they will tell us how to do that. I believe I can do this. Can you?"

"It's not a matter of whether I can," he said. "This is something I must do."

He needed this "tool for independence," as he called this animal he had decided he must bring into his life. Whatever rotting leftovers of the past he would have to discard or destroy to make this work, he would. It was that important.

A few weeks after submitting his application, he received word he'd been accepted for the next class.

⁓

Spring breezes were carrying the fresh scent of new growth over the fields north of New York City, when, in early May 1990, Max arrived on the sprawling, tree-studded campus of Guiding Eyes for the Blind, long respected for the quality of its guide dogs and for carefully sorting through every detail of a person's life in order to pair up each client with precisely the right animal.

Max was one of twelve blind or visually impaired people who had traveled from Ohio, Kentucky, Massachusetts, and several other states for the twenty-six-day training session, all of them knowing this step they were taking would fundamentally change their lives.

At sixty-eight, Max was the oldest student the school had ever accepted—though in subsequent years, increasing numbers of older people sought dogs as the result of losing their eyesight to injuries, diabetes, or other later-year diseases.

Max was also the first student who had ever arrived with a gut-gripping fear of dogs.

The age thing, school officials had assured him on the phone before he arrived, was one they would contemplate, and then they would simply deal with whatever issues might arise when he was with them on campus. They had been matching people with dogs for many years, they said reassuringly, and there was absolutely no reason to think that a man of nearly seventy would not grasp, process, and put to use all the information and instruction they would provide as completely as a man of twenty.

The dog-fear thing they didn't prepare for. Max hadn't mentioned it.

The official welcoming that first day, efficient and well-paced, fanned the interest and excitement already burbling in the people who had arrived there to be joined up with dogs—people from diverse backgrounds, positions, and pursuits, including a radio station employee, a snack-bar operator, and a college student poised on the brink of a career. When the overviews, stage-setting, introductions, and welcoming had ended, the chatter of expectation ricocheted about the room.

Max sat stone-faced.

Now is the time, he figured. He grasped his cane to approach training supervisor Charlie Mondello.

Straightforwardly and unapologetically, Max made his confession. Scared of dogs. Terrible nightmares of dogs, the result of unspeakable violence in concentration camps years ago, decades ago. Even when they were not maiming or killing, they paced, those dogs, tense and alert, straining at their leashes, always ready at a single word to leap on a man, pull him to the ground. Even pet dogs set him on edge now, triggered visceral reactions.

Charlie needed to know all this, Max told him, because it would explain why Max's behavior might be tentative or reluctant sometimes, once the dogs were around. But he would press himself to move beyond those images of the past, beyond the way his mind and body reacted to dogs, he vowed. His motivation and need were that strong.

"I am capable of overcoming this fear," he insisted.

Charlie said nothing for what seemed a long time. *This is it,* Max thought. *They will send me home. Nothing can be done for you, they will say. It is impossible.*

"No human being is born evil," Charlie said at last. "Some become evil. No dog is born vicious. Some are trained to be vicious. Give us a chance to prove to you that the dog you will get here will guide you safely, love you, and protect you."

Max softened in relief. "I will work very hard. If I fail at this, it will not be for lack of trying."

In 1990, this school was one of only four in the country that was training and placing guide dogs with blind people, and the twelve-hour-a-day schedule and curriculum had been honed over thirty-six years to make the most of every minute each crop of students spent there. There is nothing simple or casual about uniting a person and a guide dog, and it takes a significant amount of time to instruct the human side of the team in everything he or she must know to make the relationship with the dog, already trained and nearly ready to set out into the world, successful and safe.

For the first two days of preparing to be a team, as it's called when a dog and a person unite, the students had no contact with the animals. This delay was partly so the students could begin to open their minds to accepting that the two of them, person and dog, would have a relationship like no other. They would rely upon each other, support each other. They would accomplish much together, but that does not happen simply by handing the leash of an impeccably trained dog to a willing blind person.

The students would grow comfortable, during this preamble, with some of the realities of life with a guide dog, with the feel and scent of the harness they would use to work together. They would begin to come to terms with the reality that the journey to get them to the point where they could leave this place with a dog—and, just as important, with the confidence, emotional wherewithal, and skills to venture forth in an entirely new way—would require a depth of faith and commitment demanded in few other endeavors.

There was also another reason for the delay in presenting the dogs to the students.

Each animal had been scrupulously bred—Labrador retrievers, golden retrievers, and German shepherds—for the calmness, intelligence, even temper, resilience, and scores of other qualities required for a dog expected to take on enormous responsibility. Each had been plucked from its litter for demonstrating, even at just a few weeks old, the qualities critical to becoming a sound and reliable guide dog. Each had been raised for more than a year by carefully selected volunteer puppy raisers all along the East Coast, people who took the young animals into their homes and lives and hearts, teaching them good manners and some obedience skills, taking them to work and to school and to social events to acclimate them to crowds, children, traffic noise, chattering squirrels, elevators, howling sirens, noisy restaurants, and hundreds of other situations and circumstances.

Each young dog had been monitored, assessed, and tested again and again along the way—some failing to progress to the next step for any number of issues, like ball obsession or fear of escalators. (Those that didn't make the cut moved to more appropriate jobs, or to life as a pet.)

Turned over to the Guiding Eyes trainers at fourteen to eighteen months old, they were again nurtured and challenged for several months, pressed into serious training, learning the skills critical to guiding the blind, spending hours a week for six months or more, mastering obedience and also focus, and listening for commands like "forward" and "right" and "left." Again, some failed to make the cut.

Each of the dogs ready now for assignment had $20,000 worth of careful breeding and purposeful training in its background, each among the small percentage—one-third or fewer of any given litter—who had sailed through every month and every test and had not demonstrated even a small flaw along the way. Each was well-mannered, friendly, fit, and eager to work.

And yet, for all the precision and prescribed routines in their breeding, selection, raising, and training, for all the similarities in their temperament, skills, and intelligence, the dogs were far from identical. Each had distinct personality traits and characteristics that separated one from another, and it was these traits that usually made one a better match for one particular person rather than another.

The instructors already knew, from an exhaustive application process, a great deal about each student's lifestyle, family situation, living arrangements, and work and travel needs by the time he or she arrived on campus. This helped them to develop early notions about what dog would fit with which person.

Some dogs, more athletic and action-oriented, were ideal for a high-octane blind person; some, extremely cuddly, very laid-back—"plodders," as they are known—would be perfect for a low-energy person who wanted a languorous companion guide. Much of that part of the equation had already been calculated. But now, as they spent hours with the students, the instructors were learning more about the nuances of these humans' behaviors, such as their normal walking pace, and some of their idiosyncrasies. This knowledge would help to ensure that each person got a dog that would mesh naturally into a life that both parties found satisfying.

With Max this wouldn't be easy.

Two days after the students had arrived on campus, on a misty Wednesday afternoon, an excited buzz thrummed around the lunch tables. This was the day. In a few minutes they would go to their rooms, and each would wait there to meet the dog that would serve as his or her eyes for the next several years. Eleven of the students were punchy with excitement.

Max was drenched in sweat.

Knowing this would be a rough pivot point for Max, the trainers had gone to special lengths the night before to prepare him, sharing some information about the dog he would receive—a deviation from standard protocol, but important for this student, they believed. Jan Abbott, the instructor assigned to Max, had pulled him aside after dinner for a private conversation.

"I want to talk with you about the dog you will get tomorrow," she had said. "I won't tell you his name; you'll have to wait for that. But I do want to tell you these things: I know your dog. I've worked with him. He's a beautiful chocolate brown Labrador retriever, and he's a good dog, a very good dog. He's the right dog for you, and I know you will make a very good team."

Knowing some specifics about a process or event likely to induce some measure of distress can sometimes help to reduce anxiety, and Max understood that this had been the goal of these few bits of information. Now he could let these few facts brew in his mind before the actual encounter the next day. *Maybe that will help,* he thought. Also, it was not insignificant that Jan, whose direct manner and obvious depth of knowledge Max had appreciated from the moment he had met her, had handpicked the Lab.

This was information to take to bed, good to have, he thought.

Whatever part of him believed that, however, couldn't convince the part that didn't.

He didn't wring much sleep from the anxious wee hours, and what he did was fitful. Brown dogs everywhere.

And now the time had come to join up with this animal.

His room felt too hot, too close as he sat with the balls and chew bones they had given him to greet the dog and play with him as first steps toward developing a relationship. They felt a little strange, silly even, in his hand.

Max could hear the rubber-soled sounds of trainers walking dogs through the hallways, the opening and closing of doors as one dog after another was introduced. Emotions were running high, he could tell. Some of his fellow students laughed and made high-pitched baby-talk noises; some gulped out a sob when they finally felt the warmth of the animal against them, a devoted being who would be always with them, eager to participate in whatever adventures they sought, whatever routines they established.

The sounds came closer. The room felt smaller, stuffier. This was worse than he had expected. Max was next.

He heard the sound of soft padding feet, four of them, approaching. A warm leather leash was pressed into his hand.

"This is Calvin, Max," Jan said. "He is a big brown Labrador retriever."

Max grasped the leash, awaiting further instruction.

"You can pet him, Max," she said.

"Good dog," Max said, and plopped his hand onto the big dog's neck. It felt silky, but he didn't especially like having his hand there. Calvin looked at him expectantly.

Max repositioned himself into a straighter posture. "Well, soon it will be time to get to work."

Mahogany-colored Calvin, exceptionally handsome even in this crowd of extremely good-looking dogs, had been teamed up with him, Max later learned, partly because the dog was an enthusiastic walker whose natural gait was quite similar to that of the man, a matter of importance in making any guide-dog assignment. Equally important was that, although Calvin was a genial, affable sort, he had a much lower need for affection, physical contact, and murmured endearments than most Labs. This exceptionally strong emotional constitution, this get-it-done channel of resolve, the trainers believed, was the special trait a dog would need to cope with the fact that Max, although he would be kind and treat the dog well, might never be especially affectionate.

Born in January, two years earlier, of Deacon and Francie, Labradors with impressive bloodlines from outside breeders, Calvin was one of the "C88" litter. There had been seven pups, four of them chocolate males and three black females, all with names starting with the letter C. Three of them, Calvin, Claire, and Curry, had cleared every hurdle and expectation and were aiming for their assignments as guide dogs. Calvin was the most unflappable, the most phlegmatic of the three.

As the halls of the school filled with the excited babble of his classmates introducing their just-received dogs to one another, Max sat quietly, irked that something that seemed so natural and joyful to everyone else continued to be, despite determined effort, so tough for him.

This day of the dog assignments also happened to be Max's wedding anniversary, and he called Barbara late that afternoon to commemorate the date.

"The day has been very trying, but I have a dog," he said. "His name is Calvin."

"Do you think it will be all right? How are you holding up?" she asked.

"I don't know what to make of any of it."

For the next twenty-four days and nights, Max and Calvin were together around the clock, like two pieces of the same organism, walking and working several hours a day, learning to maneuver the various obstacles, risks, and predicaments that a blind man and his dog have to face together, attempting to forge the kind of relationship vital to being an effective team.

Max felt the eyes of Jan and Charlie on him almost constantly, assessing not only his ability to develop the handling skills they were teaching, but also his comfort level.

"Creating a bond is important anytime a person gets a dog, any kind of dog, even a pet," the instructors, every one of them, said repeatedly. "It is vital beyond all measure in the guide-dog relationship, where the person and the dog must put absolute trust in each other."

Max and Calvin and Jan walked the paths of the ten-acre campus and along the back roads, man and dog learning from each other, Jan regularly offering tips and suggesting small adjustments to improve how they operated together.

Every hour, many times an hour, the students were instructed and coached about the truths and realities of the dogs, what the dogs needed, what the dogs could do.

"A guide dog simply can't help a person who isn't doing his part," they heard.

The animal will not stride in and take control of a person's life; a person must contribute information. So it is important to always be confident, clear about what you want, and to signal your belief in the animal's ability and willingness to respond appropriately. The guide dog won't watch at crosswalks for walk signals but will stop if there is an obstacle, alerting the person to the potential hazard. A dog will not make assumptions about a probable destination; he must be cued by the person about where to go, and then the animal will get the person there as directly as possible, avoiding overhangs and obstacles, stopping when there is a curb or steps or torn-up sidewalk or a stack of construction material.

It's an especially tough transition, Max learned, when a person is moving from a cane to working with a guide dog. A cane is an obstacle finder, whereas a dog is an obstacle avoider. Cane users receive frequent feedback from the environment by acquiring, through the cane, information about what's ahead: changes in underfooting, mailboxes, fallen limbs. Guide-dog users not only have to place enormous trust in their dogs to guide them safely, but they also have to learn to be comfortable traveling without the same level of constant, ongoing information they received from the cane.

Even as he strained and pushed himself to grow more comfortable with Calvin as his constant companion, there was a great deal of classroom instruction to grasp, and Max was a diligent if challenging student. During lectures about risks to the dogs and to themselves, how to care for the dogs and groom them, how to tell if a dog is sick even without being able to see, he regularly questioned the instructors about their assumptions and guidance regarding dog training and behavior. This may have been due to his innate tendency to want to turn all things of an imprecise or sentimental nature into something linear and black-and-white; it may have been due to his deep ignorance of anything dog-related. Whatever the reason or combination of reasons, he insisted upon further explanation of much of the most routine information presented.

"You are speaking as if to experts. I am not an expert," he said more than once in class.

Decades of students had followed these presentations without difficulty, and some of his classmates released a quiet, smiling groan after yet another demand from Max for deeper information, clarification, or reframed explanations.

This didn't bother him. His knowledge about dogs was lower than anyone else's, and the only way to fix that was to learn on his own terms.

As days passed, the situations Max and Calvin tackled outside the classroom together grew increasingly complex, ending up finally in New York City, where they navigated busy sidewalks, rode buses and subway cars, stepped aboard elevators and escalators, and successfully met each urban challenge they encountered. These were the kinds of activities Calvin would face in Cleveland—if without quite that level of noise and bustle—and it was important that Calvin demonstrate that he was as competent with Max as he had been with the trainers before his assignment. Equally important was for Max to know that Calvin would guide him calmly through the crowds and the sirens and the distractions onto buses and into buildings when they returned home to Ohio.

Calvin gamely tackled it all, and proved that he possessed many laudable qualities.

He also proved himself a gifted food thief.

On one of their early days together Calvin purposefully maneuvered Max up the stairs to the dining room, took him directly to his place at the table, glanced around quickly to judge his prospects, and promptly snatched the hamburger resting on the plate.

Jan leapt in and corrected the dog before Max had had time to process what was happening. Here, then, was evidence of what the instructors had been talking about: These dogs are extremely well trained. They are aware of acceptable and unacceptable behavior. And, more important than either of those facts is this: They are dogs. It's important never to forget that, to always be aware of your particular dog's quirks, be vigilant about his little issues, and keep ahead of situations where these might cause problems.

"No dog is perfect," Jan reminded Max. "Each one requires a handler who is solid and alert at all times."

This was not the only time that Calvin demonstrated quick thinking and fast jaws around people food. Even before the great hamburger caper, he had managed to snatch the corned beef out of a bun—displaying a finely tuned preference for meat over bread when given sufficient time to think through a strategy. Years later he bolted down a small bowl of Hershey's kisses when Barbara turned her back for a few seconds to answer the telephone. Calvin didn't fall ill, though some dogs would have, and the silver wrappings passed through him without issue as well, sparkling in the sunshine in the midst of his droppings the next day.

A good lesson, these food thefts, Max concluded. Unexpected, as so many things about this species were. He hadn't anticipated the particularities that he and his fellow students were working through with their animals, having never thought about dogs as having personalities, especially dogs of this sort, trained, he had imagined, to be almost robotic in their obedience and responsiveness. And he certainly hadn't imagined how big his role would be in getting what he wanted from this dog.

But he was learning and absorbing as fast as the instructors could toss their hundreds of facts and tips and recommendations at him. He was adapting, and he felt he was working past his dog fear.

As the end of the training session approached, Max's classmates chose him to be a speaker at the graduation ceremony. On that late-May day, Max stood before the audience and declared that he had experienced a profound reversal of thought while on campus.

"As a survivor of World War II concentration camps I became afraid of dogs. I viewed them as terrible, vicious creatures. I know now the difference. Those people in the camps were very bad people who taught dogs very bad things. Here at Guiding Eyes for the Blind, very, very good people teach dogs very good things."

He may have thought that having spoken—and believed—those words, his transformation was complete.

It was not.

That afternoon, after much back-slapping and many congratulations from trainers and students, Max grasped Calvin's work harness, boarded a plane, and returned to his Cleveland townhouse.

Barbara, unpracticed and unsure in the ways of dogs, welcomed Calvin into her home as she had welcomed every kid from the neighborhood who had come by to visit Rich or Steve—with a quick hug and a couple of cookies. Calvin found her irresistible. He fixed upon her his most beguiling gaze, and, completely undone by his charm, she invited him up on the sofa, where he snuggled happily against her hip. With that, everything that needed to be settled between them had been, and there were no reservations on either side.

Max set about working Calvin through the handful of minor adjustments to be expected when a service dog moves into a completely new, unfamiliar environment, removed from anything familiar. He began to believe it was possible this could work out even better than he had dared imagine, that he would achieve a level of independence unavailable to him for fifty years. He was feeling positive.

But Calvin, sensitive and wise, was not.

Not long after arriving in his new home, Calvin stopped following Max's commands. The dog exited the apartment door with the man each morning, and after a few steps he usually stopped, refusing to go another step. It was shocking to both of them, this absolute abnegation, Calvin glumly ignoring Max's commands.

Barbara, stationed at the window, watched the two of them frozen in place at the spot beyond which Calvin would not go. It went on day after day, man bewildered, dog unhappy. This regular replay, she knew, must be taking an awful emotional toll not only on her husband but also on the dog, and she worried that this sudden blast of unpredictability from Calvin might disintegrate into something that could put the lives of both in jeopardy.

Sometimes Barbara walked out the door with Max and Calvin, and if she positioned herself next to her husband, a body's width from the dog, stepping forward when Max did, Calvin would move along the sidewalk as he was supposed to move. Without her—nothing.

Calvin simply couldn't bring himself to take Max out into the world. That the dog was fighting against every fiber of the breeding and training that insisted he move forward with this man was written clearly and miserably across his face, Barbara told Max.

"He's not just being stubborn, Max," she said. "He hates that he is doing this."

"I must not be handling him in the right way," Max concluded. "Obviously, the problem is me."

Max phoned Jan for advice. She had a great deal. It sometimes happens that when the guide dog and the person leave the comforting oversight of the instructors scurrying about, reassuring them, making sure everything is done exactly as the dog is accustomed to having it done, things can temporarily go a bit bad. The handler must convince the dog to work as he has been trained, must reassure the dog that belief in him is strong, that there are no reservations about his ability to do the job. Some dogs and handlers bond very fast, almost instantly, she reminded him; sometimes it can take months. This lack of a bond is what had to be fixed, she said. Calvin sensed Max's unwillingness to turn himself over, and without that, work stalls.

Jan knew that this burst of obstinacy had rattled Max; it would have had that effect on anyone, even someone without his lack of confidence in dogs. But, she said, he needed to think back to those days at the school, how well he and Calvin had worked with each other, and tap into the belief that Calvin could do the work, let the dog know he believed in him.

"Be patient," she said. "Give Calvin more time to adjust. It's extremely important to work on building that bond. You must have the bond. It's vital."

Max paid close attention, recording every suggestion in his mind as Jan emptied her enormous bag of tricks into his ear, and he promptly employed the advice.

It did no good. Calvin began to lose weight.

That's the explanation, Max thought. *The dog is sick.*

"He's healthy and sound," the vet proclaimed after a thorough exam. "The problem with Calvin is the way you are with him, Max. His behavior is a reflection of your behavior. I can see that just by watching the two of you together. You need to work on yourself, the way you are with him. You obviously have no relationship with him."

If Max could correct this, the vet predicted, the problems would resolve. Calvin would be happy. Calvin would eat. Calvin would work.

It didn't happen. The dog's sadness seemed to escalate.

As June ground into July, Charlie arrived at the Edelmans' townhouse to observe and to offer suggestions. As soon as he came through the door, Calvin's demeanor changed. His eyes brightened. His posture grew straighter. He radiated excitement. Max could instantly sense the change in energy. Though glad the dog had perked up, he didn't think this sudden change in attitude boded well for their prospects as a team.

The trainer watched the two of them together, and cut quickly to the heart of the matter. Max had not been camouflaging his fear as well as he'd thought. This, plus Max's natural reticence—a cool reserve that sometimes crusted into a frosty veneer that even an irrepressible dog could not penetrate—was confusing Calvin, blocking the bonding process. A dog like this needs to know he is connected to and liked by his partner, Charlie said; a dog like this needs to feel trusted.

There were ways to get past this, Charlie assured him. He offered several observations and many suggestions.

First, Barbara's instant connection to Calvin in the face of Max's emotional distance was interfering with Calvin's ability to develop the connection with the man he was supposed to be helping, Charlie said. He reminded Max of the admonition during his month at school that others in the family should have minimal contact with a service dog until the bond with the partner had grown solid. Because Barbara was inclined toward affection and Max was not, this was especially critical in Max's case. She would have to pull back.

Charlie also reiterated the warnings issued in class: that dogs should not be given people food, a rule that Max also had not followed, especially since he'd been worried about Calvin's weight loss. That, too, must cease. Eating half a turkey sandwich every day was not exactly fostering much interest in eating dog food, he pointed out.

The list went on.

"Be more vigilant about praising him whenever he does anything right," Charlie said.

Also, it would be extremely important for Max to work much harder to show his regard for Calvin. Play with him more, make time to have some fun together away from the specter of work. Try to infuse that flat, measured speaking manner with some warmth and melodiousness. When petting Calvin, don't be so perfunctory; lean into him and use a lingering touch.

Charlie had never really had to provide step-by-step guidance about how to show affection to a dog. He had never had a client like Max before.

Max was certain he could pull this off, now that he had been guided through scores of specifics that would allow him to present the kinds of things the dog had seen and felt from other people—the warmth, affection, and trust that would regenerate his confidence about his ability to work.

"Charlie knows Calvin. He knows what he's capable of, and he knows me. I believe that what Charlie has told me will help me achieve what I must so we'll be able to work together as we should," Max said to Barbara.

Yet, by the time Calvin had been with Max for nearly three months, the dog was willing to go only a block or so, sometimes not even that, and the animal's depression seemed even more intense.

The evidence was clear, Max decided one morning. This whole idea of having a dog had been a mistake.

"I can't rely on Calvin," he said to his son Steve. "I have tried this and tried that, and nothing works. I'm exhausted. Maybe I am not cut out to have a dog."

That this hoped-for freedom could be refused him—by a dog—was torturous. There was so much he wanted to do. Volunteer work. Explorations of the city. He had received a couple of invitations to speak about the Holocaust as a result of pieces he had written, and the speaking was something he thought he might possibly take to occasionally, on his own terms, sharing only what he was comfortable sharing. A guide dog would have made all that possible.

"I have done as they said, and still, it's not working," Max said to Barbara in late August. "I think Calvin just doesn't want to work for a man like me."

He called Charlie Mondello again, this time to propose having the dog reassigned to someone else, someone who could love Calvin enough that he would perform again in the way everyone, Max included, knew he could. It would be best for everyone.

The trainer listened quietly. He had a pretty solid sense of the strength of the man, and a very solid sense of how important a guide dog could be to him. When Max had finished detailing all that was wrong and presenting all the supporting evidence about why the reassignment was imperative, Charlie spoke.

"I will not take that dog back, Max," he said. "You have not done everything you can to create the bond with him that he requires. You must work harder."

Another week passed, Max doing everything he could to overcome his reserve, show affection to Calvin, demonstrate to the dog that he was counting on him, that he was prepared to trust him.

The sought-after shift in Calvin finally, slowly, began to trickle forth. The spark that had all but illuminated the dog in New York was not reignited, just a guttering memory of it, but, as August turned into September, Calvin started to work again, guiding Max along the sidewalks, moving as asked. The dog was shoving himself through whatever reservations he had, through his worry and his confusion, and was responding to Max's instructions.

Calvin, Max figured, was finally feeling something approaching what he needed from his partner, was finally moving toward the bond Max was offering. And if their relationship wasn't everything that others in his class were reporting they enjoyed with their dogs, he could live with that if Calvin could.

So they walked, Max inching toward confidence in Calvin's dependability, and Calvin, Max assumed, inching his way toward whatever it was that he needed.

One warm late-September morning, Max and Calvin were making their way along the neighborhood sidewalks with no real purpose other than to enjoy the final days of Indian summer. They stopped at a crosswalk. When Max heard the sounds of stopping traffic that indicated the light had changed, he gave Calvin the command to cross the street. Two steps into the crosswalk, the dog suddenly stopped and jerked backward, hauling Max with him. It took a split second for Max to process the sounds—squealing tires, a car roaring off—that had prompted Calvin to do what he did.

A driver, Max realized, had come up the side street, ignored the light, cut into the crosswalk, and would have hit him had Calvin not been with him, or if Calvin had not been paying attention, or if Calvin had not taken the steps he took.

Staggered by what had happened—and what might have happened—Max crouched and hugged the dog, the first time he had ever offered affection not on a prescribed schedule. As he pulled the dog's chest against his own, felt the silky heat of Calvin's broad muzzle against his ear, he felt some resolve or barricade inside that he'd kept shored up falling away. Strange, this feeling. He didn't quite know what to make of it.

As the man returned to his feet, dusting off his knees, and gave Calvin the forward command again, the dog seemed suddenly jauntier, more confident. Just like that. *Just like what happens when the unappreciated kid in class answers a question no one else could answer,* Max thought. A tidal shift in the time it took a heart to beat forty or fifty times.

It was something to build on. And within days it was as though there had never been a problem between them, man and dog completely confident with each other.

Maybe Calvin had finally had sufficient time to adjust, Max thought, exactly as the trainers had suggested. But that didn't seem to fully explain the difference between how Calvin had been and how he was now.

Was it possible, Max wondered, that Calvin had felt the falling away of his wall? Could the dog have sensed with the crosswalk incident that Max was beginning to believe in him, and this had sent forth the initial strands to knit the elusive bond that Max had understood was necessary but had lacked the skill or emotion to bring into being?

It was, Jan suggested much later, probably a combination of all of these factors. A guide dog has to feel a reciprocation of feeling that, prior to this moment, just hadn't been evident to Calvin, and, in truth, probably hadn't existed. Also, she surmised, it was a clear moment of teamwork that had cemented the man and the dog—Calvin did what he was supposed to do, and Max learned in a split second that he could count on the dog, and he let Calvin know that.

There are pivotal moments in every relationship. And if Max didn't understand everything about what had transpired, he knew something important had happened—for both of them.

The two meshed, and with this dog, Max experienced a new level of freedom. He could set off whenever he wished, no real destination in mind, and walk for as long as he wanted to unfamiliar places with confidence. He could leave the house at dawn if he wished, and he often did, before Barbara even awoke, and stride off the aftereffects of a sleepless night.

They covered miles, month after month, Max and Calvin, reveling in the ever-changing sounds of leaves crunching beneath their feet or of packed snow squeaking and squawking the way it does when the temperature is just right. They visited the barbershop every month, where everyone knew Calvin's name; they went to dental and doctor's appointments and lunch outings and coffee shops.

"He is my guide and Barbara's pet," Max announced to all they encountered. "He tolerates me and loves Barbara."

Max had no problem with that, he said, his tone edging so uncharacteristically close to affection that it stunned those who knew him well and recalled how he used to be. "Calvin's heart is big enough for both of us."

Indeed, the dog quickly sorted through quite a number of ways of being helpful. With the children gone and a diagnosis of emphysema added to the arthritis that sometimes flared to searing levels, Barbara needed a couch buddy when she felt sapped. Calvin gladly took on the job. He became a soft bundle of affection, as close to a lap dog as an eighty-pounder can be, nestling his head comfortingly in her lap as she watched television or read. He would awake from his nap to look into her eyes with an expression verging on adoration, and cock his big blocky head as if to ask whether she required anything else of him, anything at all.

Max; his first grandchild, Hannah; and Calvin
COURTESY OF THE EDELMAN FAMILY

He became a different dog with Hannah, the tiny toddler who brought giggles into the house, a curly-headed girl with a sparkling personality, the first of two children Steve had with second wife Janet. With Hannah, Calvin took on the role of patient, accommodating, ever-ready playmate. His tail would wave so hard his whole backside would swing from side to side as he and the girl (and later her brother, Andy) played hide-and-seek, or chase-the-dog, or whatever other games kids and dogs devise that make perfect sense to them and no one else.

It was the same later when Rich married a vibrant young woman named Sue, who had three children—"She came fully furnished," Max announced with a grin to friends—and Calvin had more little people to nurture and play with.

With Max, Calvin was a serious, skilled jobholder who relished the chance to show his mettle. The moment the working harness came out, Calvin jumped to his feet, quivering with anticipation, eager to hit the streets and do the work he was so sure of, so good at, for a man he knew appreciated and trusted him. Calvin became the ideal partner, just as the trainers had predicted, for a man of structure and routines, rules and standards.

Still, somewhere along the way, the dog—apparently concluding that Max needed a little more humor and unpredictability in his life—developed the habit of stealing Max's socks as the man was dressing. Nearly every morning, the big dog inched stealthily, silent as a fox stalking his prey, to where Max had laid out the day's clothing. When Max was preoccupied with zippers or buttons, the dog made his move, pouncing in from the side and making off through the house with his plunder.

Max, the man of habit and sequence who had never before left a task unfulfilled, would interrupt whatever he was doing and take off through the house, roaring, because that's what Calvin wanted.

—~—

Realizing that they no longer had to live directly on a bus line because Calvin could guide Max wherever necessary, including to a bus stop a few blocks away for trips downtown or across town, Barbara and Max bought a small two-bedroom house on a quiet street in Lyndhurst. Rich and Steve built a deck so Calvin and Max could sit in the shade of the enormous maple tree, and they had a fence installed around the huge backyard so Calvin could romp or relax on the grass.

It was a new neighborhood for man and dog, but they explored in ever larger squares, walking at least four miles every morning, and soon these streets grew as familiar as those of the old neighborhood. Sometimes, as they snaked their way through the side streets and cul-de-sacs, Max fell deep into thought, and the moment would arrive when he realized he had no idea where they were.

"Okay, Calvin, let's go home."

The dog would turn in the direction of home, not certain exactly how to get there, and eventually they would reach a street that Max recognized—because of the traffic sounds or the surface of the sidewalk or the familiar scent of the neighborhood bakery—and from which home could be found.

"We got home in a very unusual way, but we got here," Max would announce merrily to Barbara when he and Calvin eventually burst through the door.

With Calvin at his side, there was no chance of Max remaining closed into himself and remote when he was out and about. Neighbors saw the deep-chocolate dog and began conversations. Shopkeepers recognized them as they made their daily rounds, and would introduce themselves and call out to Max and Calvin as they passed.

Calvin was serving as what the experts term a "social lubricant"—a charming dog escorting Max, attracting attention and conversation of the sort that Max, on his own, would not have had. With Calvin, he was constructing a broader, richer life that became wider with each passing month.

Every Tuesday the two of them left home right after daybreak, headed for the bus stop, and traveled downtown to the Cleveland Library for the Blind. For the next several hours Max performed volunteer work, mostly quality control of books on tape. People in and around the library stopped to watch as the two of them passed, the trim man with the brisk pace and the handsome dog, focused, noble, always at the man's left side. After a while, those people approached, filled with questions:

"What does Calvin do while you're working?"

"I keep him on a long leash for his own safety, so if someone opens the door he cannot bolt out, but he can still wander around the room I'm in, and, if he gets tired of being next to me, he can go off in a corner and lie down if he wants to."

"How do you know when it's time to take him out for a potty break?"

"I keep Calvin on the same schedule for meals and water that he had at the training school where I got him, and this ensures that his elimination breaks are needed at the same time every day and every night, and I make sure, no matter what, to get him outside at these times."

"Does he ever get to play?"

"Yes, he does. All work and no play would make Calvin a very dull boy. He knows when the harness is on he is my guide, as he has been trained. But when we are at home and he knows it's time to relax, he can chase balls in the yard or snuggle with my wife on the couch."

Max had discovered what he regarded as an astonishing level of ignorance about how guide dogs function with their people, and he relished every chance to inform others. He was always firm in explaining that Calvin was not a pet but a brilliantly trained working animal with significant responsibilities as part of a well-oiled duo operating in tandem.

"It is a partnership. I, lacking in sight, contribute the power of reason, and Calvin, lacking the power of reason, contributes the sense of sight."

Calvin, an adventuresome sort, was fond of any outing, but he especially liked these Tuesdays downtown at the library. He had nosed out every hot-dog vendor in the vicinity, and at lunchtime he took Max directly to one of them—always getting his own little nub of meat for his trouble. Sometimes, if he was feeling particularly lucky or convincing, he tried to entice Max to visit a second vendor.

Max developed a greater willingness to speak about the Holocaust and about being blind, which resulted in a growing flurry of invitations from elementary schools, high schools, and colleges, Calvin always lying calmly a few feet away, seeming to enjoy the sound of Max's voice and the attention the man was getting. One group of fourth graders was so enthusiastic about the Max and Calvin Show, as they called it, that they organized a fund-raiser, collected $100, and donated it to a guide-dog school.

How much of this Max could have, and would have, agreed to had he not had Calvin to get him to his destinations and to be a warm presence against his darkness is impossible to know. But things were very different now than they had been in the pre-Calvin days. Max, in his seventies, was increasingly being seen as a teacher, developing a patient style and an ease with talking about some of the awful moments of his past that he had previously preferred to leave undisturbed.

Max and Calvin became regulars at a monthly program called Face to Face, in which busloads of Cleveland-area high school students were transported to a synagogue for lectures about the Holocaust. He received and accepted an invitation from a group of Holocaust survivors in New York to speak at a commemoration of the fiftieth anniversary of the liberation.

One morning, after Calvin had been with him for several years, Max was having a bagel at one of his regular spots, the dog, as always, curled at his feet. When the proprietor stopped by the table, talk shifted to the local elections.

"You should consider running for the Lyndhurst council, Max," the man said. "You're retired, you have the time, and you would do the job as well or better than others."

"Who will vote for me?" Max said with a laugh. "I am not well known in the city."

"You must be kidding!" the man responded. "You walk with your Calvin all over the city. People may not know you by name, but they all know who you are. Print campaign literature with pictures of you and Calvin, and people will say, 'Look, here's the man with the guide dog. Let's vote for him.' They'll probably vote for Calvin, but you'll still win."

Max didn't throw his hat into that particular ring. He did, however, become something of an activist. From 1998 until 2001, he served on the board of Services for Independent Living, an advocacy group aiming for total acceptance of and adherence to the Americans with Disabilities Act, which had passed in 1990 but was not uniformly or universally applied.

His volunteer work with the library grew, too. One Tuesday morning in August 1997, as he and Calvin headed for the sorting room, library director Barbara Mates intercepted them.

"There are blind children who need more practice reading and writing in Braille," she said. "The teachers don't have the time, and most of their families don't know Braille. Do you think we could organize a group of volunteers to help the kids?"

"Yes, of course," Max said, wholly unsure whether, in fact, such a group could be organized.

There were many obstacles, most of them unanticipated, but eight months later, Braille Read-Together was launched, with volunteers and willing youngsters meeting every Saturday. Max worked one-on-one with a girl who was blind and had other disabilities.

"By fifth grade, six years after she and I had started working together, that little girl read Braille faster than I did," Max proudly told his friends years later. "It is hard work, the tutoring, but it is my greatest pleasure."

At about the same time, the library installed its first "talking" computer, equipped with software called Screen Reader, which translates text into speech. Mrs. Mates suggested Max be the first student/user, even though Max had never before indicated or demonstrated any particular interest in, or facility with, technology.

William Reed, a librarian and computer expert, and, as Max later described him, "a man of much patience," taught Max to send and receive e-mail, use word-processing programs, and access the Internet. When the bugs had been worked out and the equipment made available to library patrons, users sometimes complained that learning it was too hard for a blind person. Reed always responded: "If Max was able to do it at the age of seventy-nine, anyone can."

Calvin and Max took on all of these new challenges together, a team, as close as any. People from miles around knew them. Newspaper stories were written about them. They learned from each other and taught each other, Calvin regularly surprising Max with his amazing good sense.

The two were out together on a summer afternoon when a quick-forming storm blew in with a blast of cold wind and an instant downpour. Max quickly reversed direction with Calvin, heading for the bus-stop shelter a block away, figuring they would wait out the rain there. Oddly, when they reached it and Max instructed Calvin to enter, the dog disregarded the command. It was so uncharacteristic that Max decided to see what his dog was up to.

Calvin took a sharp turn into the driveway a few steps away, and Max, knowing precisely where they were, suspected that Calvin had felt the bus shelter wasn't nearly as good a solution as the Jewish Community Center that they had visited several times in the past. Indeed, in less than a minute, Calvin and Max were standing in the lobby of the JCC, out of the rain and wind, much better protected, Max frequently told people, than they would have been if the two of them had done things Max's way.

Max by now had decided this was an animal unequaled. The trainers at the school had regarded Calvin as intelligent, though not necessarily, among his peers, exceptionally so. Max found him brilliant. Calvin's food obsession never really abated; Max regarded it as an endearing quirk. Calvin could entice the grandkids into turning a nice, quiet afternoon into a cacophony of shrieking, laughing, and dog noises; Max found this delightful. Max liked everything about this animal: his eagerness, his streak of silliness, even his big, deep bark, which sounded threatening to most people, as it had to Max in their early days, but now seemed to Max a joyful, boisterous song.

Happy in each other's company and with the adventures each made possible for the other, Max and Calvin worked and walked and traveled together for nine years.

At age eleven, Calvin developed arthritis. Medication helped, but the dog was moving much more slowly and had trouble climbing stairs or getting into and out of cars. A walk of only a couple of blocks left him limping.

Keeping Calvin moving would help his joints, the vet said, but he couldn't work as a guide dog any longer. More was required of him than he could provide, though he tried to hide his pain and act as if nothing could possibly stand in the way of getting Max where he needed to go.

Barbara had become very ill by this point, her emphysema so severe that she had to haul oxygen around in a wheeled canister. Max knew that he couldn't care for Calvin along with a new guide dog. He was also sure that it would bother Calvin to see him walking out the door for the long morning walk or for speaking engagements with another guide at his side. So he wanted Calvin to have a new home.

The dog had done his job and done it well. He had volunteered to take on additional responsibilities with the family and had performed them admirably. Now it was time for him to have the restful, happy retirement he deserved, Max told Barbara. These things happen. A dog doesn't live forever, and a guide dog can't perform for more than six or eight years. That's just the way life goes.

Max called Guiding Eyes for the Blind to say he needed another dog. Very businesslike. He asked if they would find a family to care for Calvin in his retirement. Max knew that this was what often happened when a guide dog couldn't work anymore, and, for any number of reasons, his partner couldn't continue to care for him.

School officials said they would take care of everything.

In May 1999, Max returned to the place where he and Calvin had first met. All the arrangements had been made. A family in Virginia had stepped forward to adopt Calvin; they were eager to have him finish out his final years with them, and they would love him.

Trainers had picked out another dog for Max. He would meet that dog soon.

The old man made his way slowly to the room he had been assigned for the time he would be on campus, Calvin moving at his side, guiding as he always had. Max sat on the edge of the bed and the dog moved against him, leaning against his leg as he had hundreds of times, thousands of times before, Max rubbing his ears.

How many miles had they covered together? Max wondered. Thousands, certainly. Eating out regularly, making their way into schools and synagogues to give talks, meeting dozens of people, working at the library, Max always aware of Calvin's willing presence.

A gentle knock on the door roused him.

"Max, you have thirty minutes to say good-bye to Calvin," instructor Ellin Purcell said softly.

As the minutes passed, Max sank into a sadness he hadn't expected. He remembered the sounds of Hannah and Andy squealing happily as Calvin, young then, had gently grabbed the front of Hannah's shirt and pulled her to the ground with a little thud, dog and kids rolling on the floor together, giggles and tail-thumping filling the room. He thought about all those evenings the dog had snuggled against Barbara on the couch, she humming softly, soothed and content.

Calvin, always so jolly, seemed as melancholy as Max at this moment. The dog knew every posture, every mood of this man, and he knew the man was deeply unhappy.

Ellin knocked again, entered the room, and silently attached a leash to Calvin's collar to walk the dog away. Maybe Calvin turned to look at Max one last time when he reached the door.

Max would never know.

Eight

Max received the "replacement" dog, as he had come to think of this new animal, the next day. He'd had to bring this new one into his life because, he now knew, he was a man who needed a guide dog. But this one would never be half the guide, half the funny companion Calvin had been. There was no point pretending otherwise.

This dog's name was Silas, and he was a big Lab like Calvin. This one was the color of cornstalks in a sun-splashed autumn field, and he had soft brown eyes that seemed to plumb the soul of each person he met, finding the best of whatever resided there. Born two years earlier at the school's breeding center, he was raised by gifted puppy raisers in Maryland, who had quickly seen an unusually gentle, giving spirit, even when he was a tiny thing, still clumsy and unfocused.

"He's an old soul—such inner wisdom," Jan Abbott said to Max. "Trust me. You will come to love this dog."

Silas and Max would not have been a good match in earlier years, but the Max Jan saw before her now—more tranquil, more open, more affectionate—no longer needed a stoic dog that would have to try to muscle through Max's peculiarities. These two, she felt, would get on very well together.

Max wasn't happy with the new dog at first, found things to complain about. This happens often when someone must give up a beloved guide dog and form a new relationship with a strange one. There's even a phrase to describe it: The person is having difficulty with "switching loyalties."

Max grumbled about Silas's walking pace. Jan assured him that he and Silas would make the tiny adjustments necessary to walk perfectly in step. Max complained mildly about other small matters. Jan reminded him that no two dogs are alike.

Silas would work and keep Max safe as a guide dog should, but he wouldn't be Calvin, and, in fact, he shouldn't be Calvin, Jan said. Every relationship is different, and establishing the right footing, the right emotional framework and the right communication shorthand with each one takes time, and a willingness to embrace the new dog's personality and traits.

"Remember: Patience is the glue that most effectively binds two creatures together," Jan said to Max again and again.

By the end of the training session, Max hadn't reached the comfort level with Silas that he'd achieved with Calvin, that remarkable feeling of a perfectly fitting glove, and he certainly felt no special attachment to this animal. But he left for the airport confident in Silas's reliability and work ethic. This was a gift from Calvin, Max knew—the ability to trust this new dog without empirical evidence or any shared history with him.

Watching Max walk away with the gentle golden dog, the man more erect and purposeful than when she had first met him, more open to the dogs in this session than the last, and also to the students and instructors, relaxed enough that his wry humor regularly had spilled forth, Jan thought of Calvin and smiled. *You did a great job, big boy,* she thought. *You were much more than a guide to Max. You took him to a new, good place.*

It wasn't the first time she had seen a dog-assisted transformation of a person. They are quite common in the world she inhabits. But this one, she thought, this one was especially big and special.

Back home in Cleveland, sweet-natured Silas slid competently into his work with barely a hitch, even in their earliest days together, reliable as the spinning of the planet, polite and attentive. In no time at all, the dog and the man, now in his eighties, were asserting themselves around the city, attending to business, visiting the barbershop, coffee shops, and library.

Silas learned the word *mailbox* very quickly, and made his way there, just as Calvin had, so Max could post the growing number of editorials and articles he was writing about the Holocaust and about the community of the blind, many of them much more personal and emotional, much less distant now than the earlier ones had been.

Silas was the name the dog had come with, but it didn't last long. The man who had been afraid of dogs, the man who had sought to have a dog only out of necessity, and had taken this one because it was the only way to preserve his newfound freedoms, bestowed upon this new dog a new name: *Boychick,* a Yiddish endearment meaning "nice little boy."

It wasn't a nickname; this was the dog's name. Few in Max's circle ever knew he'd had a different one.

Just a few months after coming home with Max, Boychick made his first appearance at a formal event. In October 1999, Max was honored as one of Cleveland's twenty most successful disabled people. Max and his dog, accompanied by Rich and Sue, spent the evening at Tower City for the inevitable speeches and picture taking—more of Max and Boychick than anyone else.

But long before that, Boychick had insinuated himself seamlessly into the Edelman household, having assessed the situation in minutes, just as Calvin had, and decided he would be assuming two very different roles here. His focus and behaviors shifted instantly and completely, depending on who needed him.

He spent hours beside Barbara on the sofa, always careful to avoid the plastic lines carrying oxygen from the tank to her lungs, especially mindful, anyone could see, when her arthritis was flaring, positioning himself as gently and exactingly as a woodland bird.

"How does he know, Max?" Barbara asked one pain-riddled afternoon after Boychick had fused against her side, almost as if he had no bones and no weight, a big blob of soothing warmth.

Max and Silas/Boychick
COURTESY OF THE EDELMAN FAMILY

Max couldn't explain it, and he told her so. But the dog's intuition and instincts impressed him.

By now Barbara was inching closer to being housebound, but she encouraged Max and his dog to go about their business as usual. She was content at home, she said, or, if not exactly content—because her hands hurt too much to knit or crochet as often as she'd like—she was fine. It wouldn't help anything for Max to stay at home with her when he was itching to do more, meet more people.

Max saw no point in arguing with her, staying underfoot, when she had her own patterns and routines. He and Boychick continued to visit the library every Tuesday; they did their volunteer tutoring with children, the dog so brimming with love that he made the kids feel even more supported and confident. The pair went to schools and synagogues regularly, and they walked, miles and miles, week after week.

When Barbara's condition deteriorated even more and Max insisted upon spending more time at home, writing more editorials and articles, Boychick was almost always at Barbara's side, providing a sort of comfort that no one else could. She and the dog sat quietly, happy just to be in each other's presence. When Barbara napped, Boychick watched her, worried, one paw always reaching out to make contact as if that would somehow make her breathing a little less labored.

Barbara was most serene, even as her condition worsened, with Boychick curled against her, pressing as many inches of himself against as many inches of her as he could manage. Boychick didn't expect her to pet him or talk just because he was there beside her, and she didn't feel the need to pretend she was happy or upbeat.

Max marveled at how Calvin, and now Boychick, each chosen specially for Max's own requirements and personality, very different dogs at the core, had both recognized his wife also had some needs, and had tended to them as well.

As 2003 drew to a close, Boychick, who had lived for more than four years with this woman, seemed to know, as Max did, as the whole family did, that Barbara would not live much longer. The dog's expression mirrored the humans' who arrived to surround her, all of them concerned, all of them respectful of Boychick's place at her side.

The day after Christmas, Barbara was rushed to the hospital. Ten days later, after around-the-clock vigils and hushed conversations at her bedside, Barbara Edelman, Max's wife of fifty-two years, died.

Max was flattened, and Boychick's misery seemed to match his own. Even in this awful state, Max could sense that. The house reeked of sadness, heavy and bleak. They both, man and dog, wandered apathetically from room to room, one no less despairing than the other.

Max, never able to reach out for comfort from others, didn't want people around. His sons, brothers, and friends tried to abide by that wish, and they mostly kept the distance he demanded.

Boychick did not. The dog hovered every moment, never more than a foot away from the man, lying with his big muzzle on Max's foot, leaping to his feet and following close when Max hoisted himself out of his chair to go to the kitchen for water or a sandwich. And Boychick's insistent closeness gave Max an unfamiliar sense of peace.

Still, surges of sadness sometimes slammed into Max so forcefully he was swept under, lost. Boychick seemed to know when Max had been hauled down, and he would nudge the old man, demanding his attention, insisting that the two of them leave for a walk around the neighborhood. They developed a habit of walking a mile or so to a doughnut shop every morning for coffee. Max didn't talk much to people there, but he was edging closer to the world again, and he knew that this was better than staying alone in the silent house that had once buzzed with the sounds of Barbara frying potato pancakes or cooing with one of the grandchildren.

When Max was finally able to mobilize himself into doing things other than those tasks he could handle almost by rote, he donated large-print and Braille prayer books to the temple they had joined in 1972, in Barbara's memory. A few months later, Rabbi Matt Eisenberg—aiming to demonstrate to the congregation that a blind person, using Braille, can participate fully in worship service—asked Max to read to the congregation at the Yom Kippur service.

With Boychick at his side, Max stood before the assemblage and read from the book of Isaiah. He did so every year for several more years, making the point that the rabbi and he agreed needed to be made about people with disabilities, and he was proud to do it.

One year during his recitation, Max's finger slipped, causing him to lose his place. He halted.

"Is there a problem, Max?" the rabbi asked.

"Yes; I lost the line." Then this man, always discomfited when his blindness caused attention or disruption, added: "You guys have it easy; you read black on white. I have to read white on white."

The congregation erupted in laughter.

Life was emptier without Barbara than it had been. But he could manage. He had to. People were counting on him. He resumed his schedule of writing and walking and volunteering, marking the years with his grandchildren's bar and bat mitzvahs and graduations, and holiday gatherings with family. He kept up connections, through phone calls and e-mails, with friends he had made at Guiding Eyes for the Blind, or through speaking engagements, volunteer work, and his walkabouts. His days were full.

On a perfect May afternoon in 2007, three years after Barbara's death, a face-warming day when the breezes seemed especially soothing after the stormy rage of April winds, Max and Boychick were returning home from a trip to the barbershop. Two or three steps into the crosswalk, a very busy driver with many things to attend to—in a rush, talking on her cell phone, not paying attention to lights or signs or people in the street—crashed into them. Max was tossed up into the air and landed in a broken pile on the asphalt, his dog still at his side. He could feel pain unfolding in many areas up and down his body, but mostly he was aware, relieved, that Boychick was standing and seemed uninjured.

Max would be going to the emergency room, he assumed, based on his inability to get up. As soon as the first police car screamed up, he asked the officer to put Boychick in the cruiser and call his son Rich, now a detective, to come and retrieve his dog.

As emergency personnel swooped in, Max realized he could smell blood—his own, he figured—but it was his legs that most worried him. He couldn't make them move. Many hours and X-rays later, he learned the full toll: one cracked rib, several gaping lacerations, and a badly fractured pelvis. The rib pain was ferocious, but the broken pelvis was the nastiest of the injuries.

"You'll walk again, Max," the doctor said, "but it will take a long time to get there, and there will be quite a lot of pain."

After five days in the hospital, Max was released to a rehabilitation facility to heal and learn to walk again. Two long months he stayed there, a difficult time not so much because of the pain, but because of the confinement. It was very hard to live that way again.

Max's friend Helen Frankmann, who had assumed temporary care of Boychick, saw very early on that neither man nor dog was doing well without the other. After a few days, she loaded the dog into her car for a trip to the rehab center. Boychick, who had worn an expression of worry ever since the man had been carted away from him in the ambulance, was thrilled to see Max again. His eyes lit up, and Helen saw a big Lab grin spread across his face as soon as he spied Max in the narrow bed across the room. Knowing he wasn't allowed on the bed, the big dog gently placed his front paws on the very edge so he could get his head close enough to nuzzle his man.

"Boychick, my boy."

That's all Max had to say. Boychick's big tail swayed back and forth, thrubbing hard up against the bedside table, rattling bottles and glasses. Max grasped a soft, floppy ear and smiled for the first time in days.

Boychick had sustained no significant injuries, Max had been assured the night of the accident, as the man had been on the side closest to the car when it hit and had thus absorbed most of the impact. And here before him was evidence, perky, if concerned, ready to do whatever Max needed.

Three times a week the dog arrived at the rehab center with Helen to spend an hour buoying the man's spirits as he fought to regain his ability to put one leg in front of the other when bones didn't line up well anymore and disused muscles roared.

A hardworking patient unusually practiced at pushing through pain, Max made excellent progress even though he was well into his eighties, and even though reigniting function at that age is a complicated proposition.

He was, however, preoccupied with thoughts unrelated to his recovery. He didn't want the woman who had hit him to be punished unduly because the man she had mowed down was blind. Punish her, yes; she was in the wrong. But it wouldn't be fair for her case to be adjudicated differently from the way it would have been if the person she had injured had been sighted.

"I want to communicate with the judge," Max told Rich when his son visited. "I must ask that emotion be pushed aside when the sentence is decided."

Rich had witnessed his father on a mission before. He knew there was nothing to be done but to fall in line and ride his wake, so he took dictation and delivered a letter to the judge who would be deciding the case. Max felt better. Now he could concentrate fully on doing what needed to be done to get out of this place as quickly as possible.

The judge read the letter in open court weeks later, when the case finally made its way to her courtroom. Maybe it made a difference.

Whether it did or not, no Edelman, father or son, ever heard from the very busy woman who had run Max down.

As his rehabilitation advanced and Max was able to walk on a track, Boychick was folded into the therapy, walking on Max's left as he always had, the therapist bringing up the rear, holding Max's belt to provide extra stability.

Finally released to go home, Max couldn't immediately walk as far or as fast with Boychick as he always had, which annoyed him, but far worse was the fact that he'd had to cancel several presentations and other activities. When a commitment is made, the commitment is fulfilled; anything less is unacceptable. But it could not be helped, and he and his dog did the only thing they could, hitting the streets again to build up strength and stamina, walking slowly, Boychick adjusting his stride and pace, eventually working up to their usual three or four miles a day.

Max, with Boychick at his side, gave the keynote speech for the Midwest Conference of Librarians for the Blind a few months later. The Michigan chapter also invited him to speak; he was featured on video at the International Conference of Librarians for the Blind, held in Boston; and he continued his work with a Cleveland Sight Center project called Share the Vision, aimed at people who lose their sight in later years and have adjustment problems after a lifetime of being sighted.

Max was invited to speak about the Holocaust at Kent State a few times, and spoke regularly for the Ohio chapter of a national organization called Facing History and Yourself, which promotes the teaching of tolerance, diversity, pluralism, and respect for differences. And he became involved with an outreach program for the local chapter of the American Council of the Blind of Ohio, which raises money to buy Braille typewriters, large-type or talking dictionaries, and talking calculators for blind and visually impaired children whose parents can't afford them.

In 2008 Max received an unexpected call. Johannes Ibel identified himself as a historian for the Flossenbürg concentration camp, which had become a memorial site. Ibel asked Max to verify his identity by reciting his inmate number, and, once he had concluded that Max Edelman in Cleveland was the Moshe Edelman who had been at Flossenbürg, Ibel invited him to speak at the International Youth Conference, to be held at the memorial site the following summer.

Max knew it would be an arduous undertaking, both physically and emotionally. He was, after all, now eighty-six years old. On a trip to Germany years earlier, so that Barbara could visit her family, he and his brother Sig had purposefully avoided Flossenbürg, not far away.

"There is no need to return to that place of torture," Max had declared.

He knew that this time, he had to go. He wanted to go. Maybe he had to show his face in the place of evil; maybe he had to honor all the people who hadn't survived. Ibel had said they needed him to tell his story, and he felt an obligation.

He began to make plans to return to Germany. Rich and Sue would join him on the trip, as would Boychick, so Max secured and filed all the paperwork and exams necessary to take the dog along.

He and Boychick ambled through the fall, but soon after the turn of the year, the dog suddenly grew lame. The diagnosis was a torn ligament. There was no possibility now that Boychick could go to Germany, endure the stress of the long trip and the packed-full days of appearances and visits. But Max had committed to the appearance, so Boychick would stay with Helen during those days of July.

The injury had additional implications, however. Boychick, the vet said, would have to be retired soon as a working dog. He would probably do fine as a pet, but he couldn't be required to deal with the rigors of getting a blind person around obstacles and up and down stairs on four-mile walks.

The pair cut back significantly on their errands and outings. Once again Max struggled to come to terms with the fact that he would have to say good-bye to a dog who had ushered him through so much, providing not only the mobility assistance he had been trained to do, but also a gentle sort of quiet support that Max could always feel, an encouraging presence that always reassured. There was no darkness Boychick couldn't light, and even if Max couldn't see that, he could feel it.

He had more difficult conversations with the people at Guiding Eyes for the Blind. In the fall, school officials told him, after he had returned from Germany and taken a couple of months to catch up, they would come to his home with a dog that would be the right guide dog for him. Boychick would go to Helen to live out his final years with the woman he loved in a home almost as familiar as his own.

On a sweltering July day, Rich, Sue, and Max began the ten-hour flight to Munich, driving an additional three hours to the place where so many had endured such pain.

As they drove up the long hill, the same hill that Max had climbed day after day, virtually blind, through biting snow and bitter cold to make airplane parts, Max held strong. When they passed through the gates of the former concentration camp, Rich describing what he was seeing—roll-call square, the barracks, the laundry, the kitchen, Max remembering moments in all of them—the man held himself erect, absorbing it all, stoic.

But when Rich described the old battered book bearing the names of all who had passed through the gates, most of whom had died here—beaten, gassed, hanged, shot, or starved and then hurled into the incinerator, or stacked up in a pile like debris, doused with gasoline, and set afire—and the rest, the survivors, nearly killed with cruelties beyond comprehension, Max broke down, fully and completely.

The demands made of him during the several days in Flossenbürg were great: media interviews, his own speech, a panel discussion, and six talks in three days to high school students, requiring him to resurrect his rusty German.

One of the questions a student asked was, "Having suffered so much in the Holocaust, do you hate us Germans?"

He hadn't expected such a question. Decades earlier the answer would have been different than the one he gave that day, born of time and distance.

"One of the things I have learned in the eighty-six years of my life is that hatred is not beneficial. The young generation of Germans has no reason to feel guilty for the crimes committed by your grandparents' and great-grandparents' generations. Feel ashamed, feel a sense of national responsibility, yes, but no guilt." The emphasis today, he said, should be mutual understanding, or at least tolerance. "The Holocaust must never be forgotten. Let's use it as a guidepost in our quest for a more-tolerant society."

His speaking obligations and the dredging about in the slime of his memories left him drained, but also queerly anxious and jittery. Details of incidents and moments he had not recalled for a very long time tumbled about, banging against his resolve, making sleep even harder than usual.

Still, he had no regrets. He had, in returning, done something of importance.

Flossenbürg had become a different place. It was quiet. It no longer carried the stench of fear and death, the horrid stink that he had never smelled before or after, the one that he had decided was the odor of evil.

On the plane trip home, he felt wrung dry, but mostly he felt deep sadness. For the way the world had been then. For the anguish that millions had endured.

—◦—

Back in Cleveland, after taking a few days to rest and compose himself, he leapt back into his schedule. Autumn was coming, the school was planning to send him another dog, and he had to make sure his calendar was clear.

He was surprised to discover that he wasn't feeling good about bringing another dog into his life, even though Boychick was now spending part of his time with Helen and seemed perfectly content. It seemed disloyal, somehow, to Boychick, because of all the dog had done for him. But with his guide dogs, he had carved out a completely independent life that disrupted no one else's. The dogs had brought him many other things, too, truth be told. He couldn't imagine giving up any of that. A new dog was necessary.

In October an instructor arrived with Lees, a placid animal with the right walking speed for Max. He was a nice enough dog, a willing partner, perfectly attuned to his responsibilities, but Max realized quickly that this dog wasn't the one for him. It wasn't just a case of the new dog not being the old dog.

"He's lazy," Max declared to the trainer. If not lazy in the strictest sense of the word, Lees certainly wasn't up to the three or four miles that Max still walked every morning, in addition to the regular errands and obligations that filled his calendar.

The dog went back to the school to be assigned to one of the many applicants with a life more appropriate to his constitution. The trainers went back to the drawing board. When they had the right dog, they said, they would let Max know.

Before they had time to do so, in December, Boychick suddenly became sick. He wasn't eating properly and had developed wrenching diarrhea. There was every chance it was nothing more than an intestinal upset, but Max had a bad feeling. A man knows his dog, and this seemed serious.

The veterinarian agreed to see him promptly and took his time examining the animal and performing tests. When he called for Max to join him in the examining room, Max heard something he didn't like in the man's tone, and braced himself.

"Boychick has lymphoma, Max. Incurable cancer."

Soon the dog wouldn't be able to hold down food or water, the vet said. Max could take a few days to say good-bye, but Boychick would have to be euthanized.

Max and Boychick went home to grow accustomed, if such a thing is possible, to the fact that their time together was almost done. Dogs can sense many things that people cannot, Max knew, and he figured this one, so incredibly sensitive, was aware he couldn't be with Max for much longer.

Too few nights later, soon after 2009 arrived, Max knew it was nearly Boychick's time to go. Boychick probably did as well. Max sat on the floor, took the big dog's head into his lap, and stayed that way with him all night, cradling and petting him, telling him what a fine guide he had been, what a good pal to Barbara and to himself. There weren't enough words to say what he wanted to say, or the right words, but he had to speak, he did speak, and he hoped Boychick understood.

The dog's bowels were no longer in his control, and when they loosed onto the floor Max cleaned him up gently and moved close again to hold him.

"It doesn't matter, Boychick—not at all. Don't worry," Max said. He wanted his dog to go gently, without worry or concern, knowing his partner would take care of everything, just as each of them had always done for the other.

On that same date five years earlier, Max realized, he had been similarly offering what little comfort he could, anguishing over the loss he knew would soon come . . . at the bedside of his wife in the hours before she died.

Boychick would sleep for a few minutes, and then awaken and wriggle closer, Max feeling him looking up at him, as if to imprint every inch of this man on his brain before he had to leave. Max did the same, in his way, slowly running his hand along the big, proud muzzle, the rounded curve of his head, the velvet ears.

Soon after the sun rose the next day, Helen arrived to drive Boychick and Max, exhausted, forlorn, to the veterinarian's office.

At 8:15, Boychick took his last breath, Max nearby.

A few weeks later, a trainer arrived with another dog, a yellow Lab called Derrick—a dumb name, Max announced, and promptly changed it to Duke. The two meshed well together, and Max was as pleased as the trainer with how quickly they understood each other. But at the end of the third day Duke was limping badly.

Max's vet examined the dog. Probably just a muscle sprain, he said, prescribing pills and a recommendation to discontinue training for a couple of days. The limp worsened, though, and on the second visit the vet did X-rays, discovering a congenital problem with Duke's shoulder joint. He wouldn't be a guide dog for Max, or anyone else.

Another dog hadn't worked out.

In July, seven months after Boychick died, after too many days of too-limited activities, Max traveled back to the school for another abbreviated class. There he was matched with a rangy black Lab with toffee-colored eyes named Tobin, plucked from a litter of eleven puppies born at the school's breeding facility, and raised by a Virginia Beach family. He was the only one of his littermates ultimately deemed ideal for guide work, and it was as if he had snatched a tiny particle from each of his siblings' impressive traits to bolster his own. Tobin demonstrated every quality the trainers wanted to see in a potential guide dog, but a fraction more of each across the board. Focused beyond imagination. Adaptable to the highest order. So eager when the harness came out, it was easy to think he probably thought about working while he slept.

He had the self-confidence of Calvin and Boychick, laced with a large measure of extroversion, a quality that in earlier years wouldn't have been suitable for Max, but now was fine. Tobin also had a moderate walking pace, not too fast and not too slow, like Max, and what is called a "medium" pull—Max's preference—meaning the dog neither hauls his handler forward nor keeps so tightly locked with the person's pace that almost no pressure from the animal is detectable.

Max and Tobi
COURTESY OF GUIDING EYES FOR THE BLIND

Again, Max had to contend with what he called the "not-quite-perfect glove fit" period, during which he was not as comfortable with Tobin as he had eventually become with Calvin and Boychick. He very much liked this dog, though. He liked his demeanor and his focus. He liked the way he moved and the way he listened. He liked his steady unflappability no matter what, even in the early days when a dog has many new things to process and accommodate.

He did not, however, like the name.

Tobin became the sportier, softer-sounding Tobi.

Back at home, the dog and the man bonded instantly and deeply. There were tiny adjustments, as always, as each went through the process of becoming fully comfortable and completely in tune with each other, but it happened with stunning speed. The dog made it clear in every way he could that he was intensely devoted to the man, that he was happy— thrilled, in fact—to do whatever Max might ask of him.

Max thought back to the difficult early days with Calvin, recalled thinking at the time that he simply wasn't the kind of man a dog could bond with. He hadn't been. And now this, a relationship forged, fast and intense.

Max taught Tobi the neighborhood, the locations of the mailbox and other regular stops, and in short order the dog was adeptly maneuvering Max around construction cones and puddles with confidence and ease. Tuesdays at the library continued with Tobi, as did regular appearances to speak about the Holocaust, Tobi half-dozing sometimes but always ready, at the most subtle signal, to pop to his feet and do Max's bidding.

"Come on, buddy boy," Max would say quietly, and Tobi would tremble with excitement, certain that once again this man had something great up his sleeve.

Tobi quickly decided Max's friends and family members were utterly enchanting, and he developed personalized greetings for most of them, always demonstrating his great delight at the company, sometimes wearing an expression of happy surprise, sometimes joy, sometimes something that looked very much like amusement, depending on the person and the circumstance.

Tobi, Max fully accepted, was not Calvin, the goof with the great sense of humor and the instant capacity to alter his notion of what his task was in times of varying needs, including, in the early days, how to build a relationship of trust with a man unable to contribute much at first. He was not Boychick, the exceedingly gentle soul with unmatched insight into human emotions and the ability to draw them into sharing the place of warmth and love he offered.

He was, simply and wonderfully, Tobi: an always-ready, ever-vigilant dog with a winning attitude and a laser focus on his man.

Soon after the shiny black dog entered his life, Max began signing his e-mails "From Max. And Tobi."

Nine

That Calvin, Boychick, and Tobi dependably maneuvered Max around the obstacles and dangers of life surprises no one. It's what they were trained to do. But guide dogs also provide and generate many benefits that are not strictly part of the job of getting a person from one place to another.

Sooner or later, most guide dogs—and their exactingly trained brethren, classified as "service" or "assistance" dogs (including mobility dogs, hearing-assistance dogs, and psychological-assistance dogs)—will take an action or impact their handlers in ways so far beyond what their trainers or the science can fully explain, it almost seems magical. That sort of thing occurs so regularly, in fact, that many experts and handlers now regard the bonus gifts these animals confer as part the package.

"There's training, and there's also what the dogs do that no one can really explain," says Karen Shirk, whose 4 Paws for Ability in Xenia, Ohio, has placed hundreds of service dogs to help children with a range of disabilities, from seizures to mobility issues. "You can't predict exactly how this thing, whatever the thing winds up being, will unfold, exactly what form it will take. It's very individual and situational. You can only know that the dog will zero in on a need and something will happen."

Karen herself had such an experience with her own service dog, a coal-colored German shepherd named Ben. Karen suffers from myasthenia gravis, a neuromuscular disorder that weakens muscles, including, in her case, those required for breathing. One evening she lapsed into unconsciousness at home when, upon doctor's advice, a visiting nurse had increased her medications. Ben must have concluded from her shallow, ragged breathing that she wasn't merely napping. When the phone rang, Ben knocked it off the cradle and barked incessantly until the caller realized there was a problem and sent someone.

"Ben wasn't trained to do this," Karen says, "but somehow he knew it would bring help."

Jan Abbott, who worked with Calvin and Boychick and is now an instructor at The Seeing Eye, often speaks of a German shepherd who made a different kind of on-the-spot decision. Guide dogs are trained never to jump on people, and such a dog would never jump on her own handler. But one morning when a truck hurtled onto the sidewalk and roared toward them, the dog leapt atop her woman, knocking her out of the vehicle's path. The dog didn't survive. Her handler did.

Some of the unexpected bonuses service dogs deliver are direct, life-saving interventions, but most are of a different sort, changing their handlers' lives not only through their assistive skills, but also by providing such a high level of unerring emotional abutment that they alter how the handlers regard the world, live their lives, and engage in relationships.

That this is the case is not exactly a far-fetched notion born of sterile soil. People have long recognized the life-altering effects of animals. Besotted owners of household pets—those of all species and with no special assistive training—have for centuries boasted of the healing properties or miracles their companions have wrought, rescuing them from fires or mountain lions or swollen rivers, saving them sometimes from the depths of despair, willing them back to health when medics and medicines had accomplished little.

Experts finally started to take note and seek understanding in the final decades of the twentieth century. The investigations began, and the discoveries rolled out.

Animals of all kinds—cats, goats, even fish—foster emotional and cognitive growth in children, they found.

They can serve as important balms to people in transition, such as those dealing with divorce or the death of a spouse.

Some people may find bonding with pets easier than with humans because animals are largely indifferent to their owners' material possessions, social status, well-being, and interpersonal skills.

Elderly women living alone are less lonely, less agitated, and more likely to be optimistic and engaged with future planning if they have a pet.

And dogs seem to provide benefits even beyond those that come from animals in general. Researchers have documented in recent years many physiological and psychological benefits of having a dog, including: petting a dog decreases blood pressure and anxiety; having a close relationship with a dog appears to be a buffer against stress; and dog owners have greater self-esteem, a stronger sense of security, and are often perceived to be happier and healthier.

People with service dogs accrue those benefits, of course, but possibly in ways and measures much larger. Researchers have only recently begun to explore the intricacies of the human–service dog relationship, but the findings are compelling.

Just six months after being partnered, handlers of service dogs have reported improvements in self-esteem, the ability to influence their own destiny, and in psychological well-being, as well as social integration. In another study, people with assistance dogs perceived themselves as being healthier than people without them. Hearing-impaired people rated themselves less lonely after receiving a hearing-assistance dog; seizure-prone individuals paired up with seizure-detection dogs reported a reduction in anxiety about their seizures and, over time, a 50 percent reduction in actual seizures; and parents of children with autism reported that having a service dog not only provided additional safety for the child, as intended, but the children also became calmer, and family dynamics improved.

A significant measure of these extra things that service dogs bestow may be attributable to the fact that "as dogs, in general, have evolved with us over the centuries, they've become very adept at picking up cues about our behaviors," in ways "sometimes not obvious to us," says Alan M. Beck, director of the Center for the Human-Animal Bond at Purdue University's School of Veterinary Medicine. And service dogs, in particular, probably "evolve into being better partners as the person and dog spend more time and experiment together." This may explain, he supposes, why service dogs seem especially inclined to sense and react to specific needs, though researchers have not yet discovered the precise process by which this occurs, how often it occurs, or even exactly why or in how many ways their handlers react to their ministrations.

But if some of the side benefits of having a service dog have not yet been fully investigated and completely explained, they occur with such regularity that they're considered by many trainers and handlers absolute truths merely awaiting formal research verification and insight.

An almost universal outcome of having a service dog, for example, is the enhancement to "social identity," as dogs draw their partners into richer, more engaged lives.

The "social lubricant" or icebreaker benefit of being out and about with a dog—any dog, in fact—is one that, although not yet studied among disabled people, has been repeatedly noted in other populations. There's just something about a person holding the end of a leash that makes others more inclined to approach or speak or smile, researchers have found. And many disabled people report that the icebreaker impact of their service dogs is especially profound.

"I am much cuter when I have my dog, apparently," offers attorney Natalie Wormeli of Davis, California, with a laugh. Diagnosed with multiple sclerosis when she was nine and significantly visually impaired by her teens, she received her first guide dog, Lance, a sensitive border collie, just before heading off to college.

"Lance became very popular, and by extension, so did I."

With each passing year, MS stole more of her vision and most of the capabilities of her arms and legs until she was completely blind and in a wheelchair. After three decades and three more assistance dogs—Bruno, a hulking hundred-pound yellow Labrador retriever; Nugget, a big Lab and golden retriever mix; and now Jeeves, a gentle golden retriever, all trained by Paws with a Cause in Wayland, Michigan, to be guide-dogs-cum-mobility dogs—she has developed a belief built on the certainty that comes from hundreds of firsthand observations: People are less "put off or embarrassed or intimidated or whatever specific thing a particular person experiences" when the disabled person has a dog at his or her side.

Natalie and the people she encounters move from chatting about the service dog to chatting about their own dogs, to chatting about dogs in general, to gliding into normal social discourse of the sort that simply doesn't happen often or quickly with a disabled person sans dog, she says. It's an experience echoed by nearly every disabled person who invites an assistance dog into his or her life.

Kate Lawson of New York spent her first "fear-filled" year at Goucher College in 2008, "shy, unwilling to participate in class or go to unfamiliar places." Severely visually impaired since birth, she felt "limited," she says, "and because of that mind-set, I *was* limited."

Kate applied for a dog from Guiding Eyes for the Blind, and during the summer after her freshman year was matched up with Bambi, an outgoing black Labrador retriever.

"When I returned for my sophomore year, I was shocked by the amount of attention Bambi and I received. I was used to being practically invisible, and now people were drawn to us like ants to a picnic basket. I met some of my closest friends because I was willing to be more open with others."

Another widely recognized by-product of having a service dog is an increased capacity to build and follow through with goals and dreams, in large part because of the confidence disabled people seem to gain from having these animals in their lives.

Natalie Wormeli, the California attorney, learned from her trainers that "if you're anxious in a situation, you must at least fake being confident and relaxed, because you transmit whatever emotion you're feeling through the leash to the dog, and you don't want the dog to start feeling edgy."

And so in every situation in which she might, as a blind woman in a wheelchair, have felt discomfort about a potentially negative reaction—job interviews and social outings and the like —she generated the strength necessary so as not to telegraph nervousness to her service dog.

"The discovery you make," she says, "is that if you fake confidence long enough, you become confident."

But it's more than just the boost that feigning confidence gives a person, Natalie says. There's a real, almost tangible shift in the attitude of a disabled person when she knows she is projecting an image of self-reliance and competency.

"It is quite a thing to go from being pushed in a wheelchair by someone to letting the dog help you get where you need to go in a wheelchair," says Natalie. On job interviews after she passed the bar exam, that made all the difference. "You go from being totally passive, being pushed in a wheelchair, which was the case when I was between dogs, to, when I was part of a team with a dog, rolling in and doing my part. I didn't have to ask for someone to push elevator buttons to get to the office or to open the door once I got there. The dog did those things. My attitude was so much better, and so was their [potential employers'] receptiveness."

She suspects that, without the dogs who have ushered her through what has become a successful career, she might have pulled back before she even started, pursued something else that required less people contact, less venturing out.

Even as her physical capabilities diminished steadily during the years, each dog, without fail, altered his ways of working with her and supporting her to meet her ever-changing physical and emotional needs. They didn't go back to school to learn new skills to help her. "They figured out how to adapt to me and for me."

Disabled people tackling challenges on a much higher level than previously thought possible, as Natalie experienced, is, in fact, common among many who get service dogs.

Kate Lawson and Bambi navigated the subways and buses of Manhattan with such ease during college breaks that she decided to take a semester abroad to study psychology at the University of East Anglia in England, a prospect that before Bambi would have seemed impossible, and after Bambi was "exciting."

Yes, Bambi did the job she was trained to do, but something happens to the heart and soul of a person who finds herself no longer alone in the near-dark. It's hard to put into words, Kate says, but the mere presence of this creature, always cheerful, always willing, takes a great deal of the psychological weight of the disability away.

Indeed, it's widely acknowledged that disabled people often experience a lightening of spirit when paired up with service dogs. Part of that, though not all, comes from being able to rely less on other people for the routine tasks of daily living.

"It's draining to have to ask for every little thing. It wears you out emotionally," says Natalie Wormeli. "I have such limited ability in my hands now that I can do very little on my own. Of course I have to rely on others. But I can prioritize what I have to ask from them, and for all the rest, from opening doors to picking up things I drop, I can rely on Jeeves. It may sound small, but it's huge if you are living it."

No less numerous are the examples of how service dogs have becalmed and softened disabled people, many of whom had erected seemingly rock-hard and impenetrable self-protective emotional barriers before their dogs arrived. Even Kate Lawson, an upbeat young woman, struggled with anger in high school. "I felt comfortable with my visual impairment, but people around me weren't, and that was a constant friction I felt." The choler trickled away like a slow-moving brook after Bambi came into her life. "I live a much fuller life, much more immersed, in part because I let go of that earlier stuff."

That service dogs squire in all of these additional benefits beyond their primary purpose has become fairly widely acknowledged in recent years, even in research circles, although "the mechanisms by which all of this transpires are unknown in many cases," says UC Davis School of Veterinary Medicine professor Lynette Hart, who has been studying the complex interplay of people and animals for many years. "Anyone who is somewhat socially isolated, who may have some medical problems, both of which can often be the case with disabled people, can feel profoundly alone. The ways in which service dogs reduce that can be quite similar and yet very specific to the individual, and that's an interesting phenomenon worthy of study."

Even the US government is intrigued enough to want to know more about the unique aspects of service dogs' relationships with, and therefore perhaps heightened sensitivity and sense of obligation to, their handlers. In 2011, the US Department of Veterans Affairs launched a three-year clinical trial aiming to place service dogs with 350 veterans with post-traumatic stress disorder. The goal is to ascertain whether the beneficial impact on the veterans' mental health and quality of life is as dramatic as many are reporting, and, if so, why exactly it happens, and whether having such a dog reduces—as appears to be the case—the costs of health care and mental-health care.

Vietnam veteran Raymond Galmiche of Navarre, Florida, who has battled PTSD for decades, recently found some relief from the horrific flashbacks and spirit-shattering anxiety that had plagued him for so long he could hardly remember what it was like to do normal things like a normal man. His balm is a big, hardworking, ever-happy German shepherd named Dazzle, trained by Guardian Angels Medical Service Dogs of Williston, Florida, which is participating in the VA study.

Dazzle did for Raymond in a few months what a loving, supportive wife and years of therapy simply couldn't accomplish, he says. "I don't think any more about 'running away'"—his term for suicide.

When he begins to descend into one of his regular flashbacks of carnage and the stench of gunpowder and seared flesh, the German shepherd, sensing the shift, leaps to his feet and licks and nudges the man—his face, his hand, whatever he can reach—to pull him back to the present. When nightmares hit, Dazzle positions himself on Raymond's chest and wakes him, cutting off the spiral before it reaches the point where the man cannot haul himself back out. Even in the course of daily waking life, when Raymond becomes anxious in the way that all people do—when he's trapped in the maze of automated voices that passes for customer service these days, or when storm winds are so fierce that trees fall and power goes out—the big dog notices and moves in with what Raymond swears is a grin.

These actions are what the dog was trained to do—to detect infinitesimal changes in the man's expression, focus, posture, and breathing, to take steps to shift his attention, to block the spiral.

But Dazzle's presence helps in ways beyond the specific duties he was trained to perform, Raymond believes. Dazzle is "completely nonjudgmental." He's never upset when PTSD disrupts schedules or activities, or interrupts sleep. Dazzle looks at Raymond, no matter what, as if he's the "most important person in the world." All of this makes a huge difference to a man battling to make, and keep, his place in a postwar world.

He distances himself emotionally from loved ones and strangers less frequently; he ventures into public more; he goes to therapy sessions only a few times a year now instead of weekly, as he once did, just to put one resistant foot in front of the other.

His war guilt—"the things I had to do to defend myself and my comrades"—is diminishing, and he is learning to trust, to shed his anger. He wants desperately for every vet who suffers similarly to be able to make the same kind of progress he has made.

"Dazzle," says the former soldier, "has my back. It's probably impossible for anyone who hasn't lived with PTSD to understand how important that is."

"It's so powerful to see these people, who had viewed themselves as a shell of what they used to be, get their dogs and take on life again," says Guardian Angels founder Carol Borden, who partnered Raymond with Dazzle and is training many of the PTSD assistance dogs that are part of the VA study.

With the increase in the types of assistance that these dogs are being trained to provide, the number of service teams in the United States has swelled to as many as 40,000. (Estimates vary widely because there is no central registry, and huge numbers of training facilities are cropping up, along with a number of self-trained service dogs joining the ranks.) As their numbers have grown, so too has the motivation to learn about the myriad ways these relationships evolve. Scores of research projects are in the works.

Still, some of what is regularly referred to as "the magic" may forever remain unexplained, even in the face of investigation. Service dogs have had an impact in ways that can probably never be deciphered.

Karen Shirk of 4 Paws for Ability trained a service dog several years ago for a child with epilepsy. During the many years the girl had the dog, trained to alert to seizures and interrupt the behaviors, she never again had another seizure. When the animal died of old age, the seizures resumed. "Nobody knows why," Karen says.

Carol Borden, of Guardian Angels Medical Service Dogs, regularly speaks about a veteran who had multiple psychological issues and medical conditions, including hugely fluctuating extremes in body temperature that he couldn't control, and of which he had only a dim awareness. One winter night while he slept under piles of blankets, his body temperature shot up dangerously. Instead of running downstairs to alert the man's wife, as he was trained to do when the man fell into one of his many medical crises (overheating not among them), the German shepherd service dog jumped on the bed and pulled back the covers, something he seemed to have figured out on his own. The dog began barking only after he had taken the necessary and instant action to save the man's life.

The man's wife rushed in just as the dog was yanking off the last layer, her husband in urgent need of a cool bath to bring his temperature down.

Jennifer Arnold, who founded Canine Assistants of Milton, Georgia, and has placed more than a thousand specially trained dogs, tells of a young woman with ALS (Lou Gehrig's disease) who requested a service dog in the 1990s. She received one, even though the life expectancy for people with ALS is usually two to five years from diagnosis. That was sixteen years ago, and the woman now has her second service dog. "Dogs," says Jennifer, "can have an extraordinary impact," sometimes impossible to explain.

When Max Edelman, now experienced in the ways of service dogs, hears about or reads these kinds of stories, he's not surprised. His dogs have granted their own special dividends that, although not as bold and dramatic as some, have changed his life in small ways and large. Ever the pragmatist, he refuses to be drawn into fanciful talk about the magic of dogs and has no interest in getting to the bottom of every factor and every mechanism that came into play in his own case. He's grateful for what he has been given by Calvin and Boychick and Tobi, much of it unexpected, and content to regard it all as one more conundrum in a life filled with them.

His former instructor and now friend, Jan Abbott, is as careful with words as Max is, but she doesn't mind suggesting that all that has happened with Max, starting with Calvin, is something pretty close to a miracle.

Max dislikes labels, but he acknowledges that his progression from a closed-in, dog-fearing man to a social, in-demand narrator with a dog he cherishes always at his side is, at the very least, a marvel. He had a role in that progression, of course, but the dogs offered the ways and means and a good measure of leavening.

If that's the stuff of mystery and legend, so be it.

Ten

Ninety years he has been on this Earth, and Max Edelman in 2012 is still shoving through life with fierce determination. He continues to prize and guard his freedom even more than most, and lives on his own in the modest house that he and Barbara bought twenty years ago. He and Tobi.

The two of them head out early every morning for a brisk, companionable, hour-long walk around the neighborhood, no matter the weather, excepting ice or sleet, which traps them inside, unhappy, Max the more unhappy of the two.

Breakfast when they return is at the little kitchen table where Max has eaten thousands of meals, and every morning, without fail, the old man slides a ripped-off chunk of toast and a piece of banana to the dog at his feet, precisely the behavior experts at Guiding Eyes for the Blind had warned against because it can turn a service dog into a food hound who noses along restaurant tabletops in search of left-behinds. Tobi sometimes does this, though he never snatches anything, content apparently with the discovery process.

Rules are rules, Max says with a wry grin, but "a man shares his food with his friend."

The two amble out the back door to the deck after the breakfast dishes are washed so Tobi can fetch balls in the huge, fenced-in yard. After he has proved his ferocity by threatening a sufficient number of squirrels and scooping up several low grounders, he shakes energetically, bounces up the deck stairs, and pads over to sit at Max's knee for his daily brushing.

"He's no good as a watchdog," Max declares with the affectionate tone used by longtime friends who recognize and point out every shortcoming but in all truth don't care about the imperfections. "Won't bark to tell me someone is at the door. They must have had a dog that barks they could have given me." He's rubbing Tobi's ears while complaining about this unfortunate deficiency, and the dog is looking straight into the man's face, tail wagging.

The two have been together for three years now, and they know each other as well as any two creatures can. There's rarely a moment they're apart, and Tobi has enthusiastically embraced everything Max enjoys most, seeming to relish all of it every bit as much as Max—visitors to the house; lunches and dinners out, Tobi curled into a tight circle under the table, motionlessly awaiting the tidbit he knows Max will eventually sneak to him; and long walks around the neighborhood. They still walk miles every day, striding purposefully through the streets, rarely following the same route twice, as that would be less interesting for Tobi, and, really, not so much fun for Max, either.

Max has an uncanny, almost mystical ability to remember the names of hundreds of streets, and their precise distance and orientation from one another, even though he has, of course, never seen them, or a map of them. No one can explain how he can visualize and recite the street grids of neighborhoods he's only walked along or heard about but never seen, but he can, and it can't be argued.

He's a man of routines partly because that's his makeup, and partly because he has quite a lot to do, and keeping organized ensures that everything gets done. As he makes his way around the house, preparing meals, tidying up, returning phone calls and e-mails, Tobi curls up in an out-of-the-way corner, awaiting any signal that he can be of use. National Public Radio provides all-day background noise. Max believes these radio chatterers can't hold a candle to the real newsmen of the past who understood news, had a commendable command of the English language, and were possessed of rich, memorable voices infused with authority and intelligence. Still, the thready, self-important voices of the NPR people filling up the house sound better than whatever racket the television might offer, he figures. He has almost no interest in TV, though he does turn it on every evening to listen to the news—more out of habit than the expectation of gaining any information of any consequence. "Again, not worth the bother," he mutters when he shuts it off.

Max spends a good part of most days in the guest bedroom/office, working at his computer, which is outfitted with software that turns e-mails into spoken words, or absorbing yet another talking book. He belongs to a reading club—computer friends who discuss a range of books, some of them best-sellers, some not.

He's a discriminating reader but not a snob. Any tale well told with good pacing and good description, regardless of whether it's sold in the literature section of the bookstore, pleases him. He has found particular delight recently in *The Soloist,* the Stieg Larsson trilogy, and *In the Garden of Beasts,* which focuses on the travails of the US ambassador posted to Berlin during the early years of Hitler's reign. Tobi, during all of this reading and computer conversation, lies in one of his two favorite spots nearby, raising his head from his doze when Max shifts position.

Some days Max might have a morning speaking engagement, a doctor's appointment, or, as he does on every Tuesday, a commitment of several hours of volunteer work at the library. The tiny shift in the dressing routine and the pace with which Max moves alert the dog to the fact that this is an outing morning, and Tobi is instantly more watchful, awaiting the moment when Max pulls out the leather working harness and says, "Let's go, Tobi." Dog and man perfectly match their pace to each other and maneuver out the door, down the driveway, and into the waiting car or cab, or they walk the few blocks to the bus stop.

"Tobi really enjoys bus rides," Max offers. "The other dogs were fine with getting on the bus and going where we needed to go, but Tobi very much enjoys it. He sits next to me, very alert. He is always watching people get on and off the bus. I think he must like all the movement and different people. I don't know."

Several times a month Max has lunch or dinner out with a friend or relative, and every Sunday afternoon, son Steve delivers the week's groceries, reads to his father any mail that has arrived, and takes care of financial matters. Then the two men and the black dog climb into Steve's car to make the short trip to his house for a family supper in the big comfortable kitchen. Tobi joins Steve's dog in the backyard to play, both disinterested in all the human conversation. But after a few minutes, Tobi makes it clear he is unhappy that Max is on the other side of the glass, without him, and he insists upon coming in, trotting through the door to take his place at Max's feet.

Max rarely misses a family event. An honored-elder presence at family gatherings, Tobi always at his side, he also joined Steve's and Rich's families for a two-week trip to Israel three years ago, a hideously hot and muggy trip that he nonetheless enjoyed. He keeps a framed picture from that vacation on the wall next to the front door, a photo he can't see, but which has been described often enough he almost thinks he can. He enjoys having it there, thinking about it being there, the family together in the Promised Land. Tobi didn't go on that trip, as the distance and horrid heat would have been too much, Max believed.

Max has become fairly accepting of the limitations and frustrations of old age, having decided it makes more sense and takes less energy to be philosophical than to rage against whatever it is that unhappy old people rail against on a given day. He broke a tooth a few months back while chewing nothing more threatening than a piece of nut bread, and that required two trips to the dentist and a crown.

"Things wear out, including teeth, I suppose," he shrugs. "Such is life."

He has some bad days, raging stomach upsets mostly, and most of the time, when it's not too bad, he simply muscles through, hopeful that time will solve the problem. Sometimes that works, sometimes it doesn't.

In January 2012, he spent a few days in the hospital after several days of feeling weak and lethargic. His hemoglobin count, doctors discovered, had fallen alarmingly low.

"Don't worry, I'm not ready for the coffin yet," he declared. The doctors did many tests. "I'm leaking somewhere, but they can't find out where."

Max bounced back.

Arthritis keeps him in a fairly constant state of dull pain, principally in his hands, the result of all those war years of chopping wood, loading timbers, and digging trenches in frigid temperatures. In idle moments, especially when reliving tough memories, he rubs constantly at his left wrist, the one with the tattoo. That's not a subconscious gravitation, he insists when asked.

"It is worse in this left hand because it is the one I use to grasp the dog's harness."

He seems somewhat more relaxed than perhaps he was in his earlier years, comfortable with his life and the patterns he has established, proud of what his sons—one a police chief, the other the chief operating officer of a large company—have accomplished.

"Both of my boys recognized I was not in a position to open any doors for them," he says. "They had to do everything on their own, and they did."

Ever phlegmatic, he doesn't effuse over their accomplishments, but he does slip into a softer, warmer tone as he speaks of them.

"They respect everything, both of them. Every belief, every person, every idea. That is what Barbara and I taught them. Respect everything. And that is how they are."

Talk of his sons reminds him of something else, a not-pleasant memory, and his voice shifts to flat again, ribbed with pain. "One time, a friend of Steve's asked him what it is like to have a blind father. Steve answered pretty fast. 'I don't think about it. He's the only father I know.'"

It's still a raw place, this bank of memories of what his sons had to endure. Tobi detects the small shift in Max's voice as he recounts this unhappy episode, and instantly jumps to his feet, moving to the man's side, nosing around until Max cups his muzzle with one hand and rubs his head with the other. It's easy to see when a person knows how to comfortably pet a dog, and this man, who once did not, now does. They both seem to relax, the man and the dog, gaining mutual comfort from the nearness and the touch.

Max still doesn't sleep well. Insomnia may be the predictable bane of every person's elder years, but for Max it's far more dramatic than that. He wakes many nights now, just as in his earlier years, sweating and panting, heart hammering, wrenching himself from the obscenely vivid images of stacks of dead bodies in a long ditch; of a doomed man standing quietly on a tall platform, hands tied behind his back, lips moving in prayer as a noose is slipped over his head; of two blond guards coming toward him, putting the whole weight of their bodies into raising their whips and bringing them down again and again on his head; of big German shepherds, eager, prowling.

Some things change with age; some do not. It helps to have Tobi there during those nighttime horrors, he thinks—calm, not at all put out when Max's troubled wanderings interrupt the dog's sleep, too.

Max is no closer today than he was six decades ago to understanding why he edged close to death in the camps so many times and survived when so many died. He has been asked the question he cannot answer so often that it seems to annoy him a little, a riddle for the ages he would like very much to solve, but cannot.

"How did I manage to survive in a Nazi concentration camp after being blinded, at a time when thousands were dying every day? A simple answer might be 'By the grace of God.' But who is naive enough to take that literally?"

There must be, he believes, a better explanation—but he doesn't know what it is.

Luck? He rejects that, too, attempting to initiate a semantics debate.

"What is 'luck'? Is winning the lottery luck? Or walking away from a car accident without a scratch luck? I do not really know. We managed to elude the rifle barrels and the crematorium fires long enough. That is as much as I know."

One explanation for his survival, advanced by a girl named Sarah, who sent him a thank-you note after he spoke to her ninth-grade class, seems as plausible to him these days as any. "There is no doubt in my mind you had a guardian angel," she wrote.

He has grown fond of that explanation, thinks it has merit. How else could he have been so close to dying, more than once, six or seven times really, and yet lasted long enough to be liberated?

The pragmatist in him also credits his brothers; Erich, the German supervisor who risked his own life for a blind Jew; and the German eye doctor, Wesseli, who saved him from almost certain suicide and became a cherished friend; and Barbara, who "made life worth living." Three of the most important, Germans.

Erich's actions are especially confounding when he thinks back, as he often does.

"Erich was fully aware of the consequences had the camp officers or guards found out that he was protecting a blind inmate, and a Jew at that. Both of us would have been hanged before the day was out. Erich took that chance. He also prevented me from taking the easy way out, giving up on life. 'Hope is the only thing we have,' Erich told me. 'Deliverance might come tomorrow or the day after tomorrow.'"

Erich, Max learned from the man's family several weeks after their liberation, died the day after he and the three Edelman brothers hugged at the farmhouse at the end of the eight-day march away from Flossen-bürg. A group of Ukrainian former prisoners launched a grudge attack and beat him to death.

Max struggles still with his long-held conviction, now confirmed by most historians, that the world was fully aware—and chose to ignore it—when the Nazis moved from bully behavior to mass murder. It's not inconceivable that such a thing could happen again today, in a different place with a different group of people, he says.

That concern has intensified in recent years as the rhetoric in this country and others has grown more acidic, more divisive. So many people have become so convinced of their own rightness that they're incapable of hearing others' perspectives. They increasingly seek out, online and through the media, only the ideas, opinions, and feelings that mirror their own. It all feels sickeningly familiar to Max, and the ache he gets in his stomach and in his heart is similar to what he felt as a teenager in Krasnik all those decades ago, when the rumors and fears began to build.

"The late Rabbi Abraham Joshua Heschel, recognized as one of the great theologians and philosophers of the twentieth century, once asked an audience during a speech, 'What is the opposite of good?' Most of the people replied 'Evil.' 'No,' Rabbi Heschel said, 'Evil has no opposite. Evil stands alone. The opposite of good is indifference.'"

When Max speaks publicly about the Holocaust, it's not, he says, "to arouse sympathy or pity for the humiliation and suffering inflicted upon us by the evil Nazis, but rather to make the world understand the enormity of evil, and to pledge to prevent history from repeating itself against any group anywhere in this world of ours."

So he talks. Even after all these years, he finds that speaking about what he lived through from 1940 to 1945 makes sleeping even tougher than usual. Stirring up the kettle of memories, hauling one out to discuss, seems to give that one or several of them additional potency for a few hours or days.

"Well, no one ever told me life would be a bed of roses," he says. Eventually he settles back into his version of normal.

A man not given to pride—a person who lolls about basking in such things is, of course, not much of a person at all—he does allow himself some small measure of smugness on one matter, and one matter alone: Despite overwhelming odds, the Edelman name has continued—flourished, in fact. That's something he and Sig, who rarely spoke of their years in the camps, talked about from time to time, when they were alone in their last years together before Sig died in 2007, at the age of ninety-seven. The silence between them would extend and then grow somehow warm, and one of them would say: "He did not succeed; he did not obliterate every Jew, and he did not obliterate the Edelmans." Hitler, they would be speaking of. He killed millions, but the Edelman brothers survived, and in their time gave rise to more Edelmans, all smart, all solid contributors to the world.

Sig, who established a successful locksmith company and survived three wives, all taken too young—one by the Holocaust, one by cancer, and one by heart attack—fathered two and raised three more when he married their mother.

Jack, a much-in-demand tailor in New York for decades, and wife, Violett, had three children. He died in 2009 at ninety years old.

Max and Barbara, with all those hurdles to clear, did better than many parents with practically nothing blocking their way. Their two sons matured into involved parents, respected community leaders, and successful career men. They're close, the brothers and their families, living a few miles from each other and from their dad. Max has special connections with his grandchildren, celebrating every holiday and every victory with them. "Grandmother Barbara and your great-grandparents Abraham and Sarah rejoice with us from Heaven," he almost always announces at their successes.

If a man's value can be measured at least in part by the contributions his progeny make to this world, this one has special worth.

People often ask whether he has regrets about moving to America. He does not. Not anymore. He worked hard to find and make his place here, and he raised his sons without fear that they would be jailed, beaten, or minimized because they were Jews. Living without fear of persecution is as precious a gift as he had imagined as a child, when he couldn't fully envision what that would feel like.

"Freedom must be protected and defended," he says, and even now, at this age, he would do whatever necessary, "with everything I have in order to protect it for my children and grandchildren."

Max is no longer the man he was when he left Germany. He's not even the same man he was twenty years ago. He is, among other things, a little more mellow, softer.

Age sometimes does that to a man. Some think that Calvin, Boychick, and now Tobi have contributed as well. Even unsentimental Max gives a little credence to that.

"At first, getting a dog was just about mobility, being able to get around. I needed a better way to do that," he says. And then, gradually, things began to happen that he hadn't expected: Calvin's and Boychick's devotion to Barbara, changes in himself, changes in the way he approached life. He doesn't understand all of what happened, but he recognizes a lot of it.

"I was uptight before I got Calvin. Very uptight." With the brown dog at his side, with the safety and companionship that came from believing in Calvin, he found himself unclenching, slowly, but undeniably. "I did not know that an animal could do that much."

He doesn't declare a favorite from among Calvin, Boychick, and Tobi. "Each dog lived under different circumstances," he observes.

He does know that Tobi is the most deeply attached to him. Barbara had passed away by the time Tobi came along, so "There was never somebody else living here for him to share his attention with."

That is a contributing dynamic, no doubt. And yet, how does one explain the fact that no open door will cause Tobi to seize the opportunity, as Calvin and Boychick did, to run off for a moment to explore on their own? How does one explain that Tobi is so devoted, he truly will not let Max out of his sight?

Max doesn't try. "I'll leave that to the experts, the people who know about such things."

Max worries about little these days, his concerns limited mostly to whether he'll feel well enough or live long enough to fulfill a commitment to speak at a high school next month, or whether storms tomorrow will disrupt his morning miles with Tobi.

Everything else he accepts as layering to a life lived longer and better than he dared hope when he was swept into a particularly nasty piece of history.

ACKNOWLEDGMENTS

A book of this sort requires much in the way of guidance, recollections, and encouragement from others.

I wish to thank Jan Abbott, the trainer who instructed and encouraged Max Edelman and his guide dog Calvin at Guiding Eyes for the Blind. Jan, now a trainer with The Seeing Eye in New Jersey, kindly spent hours recalling important and funny moments of Max's early days with both Calvin and Boychick.

Special thanks, too, to Linda Chassman, whose unique Animal Assisted Therapy Programs of Colorado augment traditional counseling techniques with assistance from dogs, cats, horses, and goats. Linda provided early direction on research regarding animals' impacts on humans. Lynette Hart, professor at UC Davis School of Veterinary Medicine, who has conducted and overseen research into the human-animal interaction for decades, also gave generously of her time, offering invaluable insights and contacts. Alan M. Beck, director of the Center for the Human-Animal Bond at Purdue University's School of Veterinary Medicine, was also a great resource.

Several people with disabilities spoke frankly and passionately with me about their lives with and without service dogs, and their stories were vital: Vietnam veteran Raymond Galmiche, attorney Natalie Wormeli, and college student Kate Lawson. Also critical were insights shared by founders of three of the dozens of organizations that train service animals: Karen Shirk of 4 Paws for Ability, Carol Borden of Guardian Angels Medical Service Dogs, and Jennifer Arnold of Canine Assistants.

Others also took the time to offer important information, including Joanne Wilson of the National Federation of the Blind, who provided vital context, as did, of course, Guiding Eyes for the Blind, the organization that united Max with Calvin, Silas, and Tobi, and provided details about those dogs and Max's training sessions at the school.

I am also indebted to Linda Kauss, friend and editor at *USA Today*, who became an instant champion of my writing about pets for the newspaper nearly a decade ago, thrust my work onto the Life pages at a time when newspapers weren't routinely writing about animals, and marshaled support to launch my weekly column. And to copy editor Patrick Richards, who took a personal as well as professional interest in my columns and gave them the full force of his skill and attention week after week. Their backing nourished my ability to report on matters of animal welfare, which eventually led to my meeting Max.

Sincere gratitude to Pam Bella, a great and wise administrative assistant during my years as an executive, now a great and wise friend, who instantly raised her hand to transcribe dozens of hours of gut-wrenching recordings of Max's memories. To my pal from Cincinnati days, Carol, who insisted that this book be written. And to my many friends and family who were instantly interested, constantly supportive, and perpetually forgiving of my absences from gatherings, dinners, and contact, including Caroline and David, Nikki and Pat, Ronni and Joe, and Ginny, my early-morning, mind-clearing hiking partner.

Finally, my most heartfelt thanks to Max, a man of unmatchable integrity and courage, for the countless hours he spent reliving painful memories and trenching deeply for details he has worked for decades to move beyond. He is an ever-achieving, ever-evolving man who, even at ninety years old, forges forward with determination, compassion, and hope. And also to his wonderful sons, Rich and Steve, and their families, who not only supported this project, but were warm and hospitable.

About the Author

Sharon Peters has been a journalist for more than three decades, writing about or editing a range of topics from politics and education to fashion and society trends. In 2005, soon after Hurricane Katrina, she took a one-month leave from her position as executive editor of a large Colorado newspaper to volunteer in southern Mississippi, part of which involved working with an overburdened, overcrowded animal shelter.

Two months later, she quit her job, returned to the Mississippi shelter twice more as a volunteer, transported several dogs from certain euthanasia there to new homes in the North, and began writing about pet issues. She launched the popular weekly Pet Talk column in *USA Today* and received body-of-work awards from the American Humane Association and the Humane Society of the United States.

She interviewed Max Edelman for a story for *USA Today* in 2009, and the two developed a friendship, which eventually led to this book.

Born in Washington, D.C., and raised in Maine, Peters has lived in states across the nation, traveled throughout South America as the wife of a diplomat posted in Colombia, and has worked as a media consultant for newspapers throughout the country. An avid hiker, she lives in Colorado.